SHED STYLE

SELINA LAKE
SHED STYLE

DECORATING CABINS,
HUTS, PODS, SHEDS &
OTHER GARDEN ROOMS

WITH PHOTOGRAPHY BY RACHEL WHITING

RYLAND PETERS & SMALL
LONDON • NEW YORK

Senior designer Megan Smith
Senior commissioning editor
Annabel Morgan
Location research Jess Walton
Head of production
Patricia Harrington
Art director Leslie Harrington
Editorial director Julia Charles
Publisher Cindy Richards

First published in 2020 by
Ryland Peters & Small
20–21 Jockey's Fields
London WC1R 4BW
and
341 E 116th Street
New York, NY 10029

www.rylandpeters.com

Text copyright © Selina Lake 2020
Design and commissioned photographs
copyright © Ryland Peters & Small 2020
See pages 156–157 for full picture
credits.

10 9 8 7 6 5 4 3 2 1

ISBN 978-1-78879-182-3

A CIP record for this book is available
from the British Library.

Library of Congress CIP data has been
applied for.

Printed and bound in China

CONTENTS

INTRODUCTION

Escaping to your very own garden retreat is one of life's greatest pleasures.

Whenever I'm invited into a shed or other garden dwelling, I can immediately see the styling potential that lies within the space. In fact, even before I step inside, I'm often in raptures over even the most humble of exteriors. I actually get a little giddy when I have a shed, summer house or greenhouse to style, as these are the places where I most enjoy working my styling magic.

As a stylist, I am often asked where I find ideas for my projects and commissions. I can honestly say that, more often than not, it's gardens and their contents that bring me the most creative inspiration. Perhaps this stems from happy childhood memories of my Nanna Doreen showing me around her potting shed in her garden in Bournemouth, watching Nanna and Grandpa Lake soaking up summer rays in comfy chairs inside their summer house, or playing with my sister in our parents' greenhouse in the 1980s. These days, my own shed is the place I like to hang out when I have free time (see pages 66–69). In this book, I'm thrilled to include it alongside the work of other designers, gardeners and stylists, making *Shed Style* a true creative collaboration.

In recent years, in line with my previous book *Natural Living Style*, I've become mindful of using sustainable materials, being in harmony with nature, making use of items I already own and buying second-hand rather than new. I'm excited to include lots of ways of using recycled materials and objects in *Shed Style*. I also share styling tips on how to make the most of any garden building, no matter what its size or function. You'll find ideas for different decorative styles, suggestions on how to furnish and accessorize any garden retreat and lots and lots of inspiration. Here's hoping you get the same giddy feelings as I do when you contemplate *Shed Style*.

CREATIVE INSPIRATION
Need some ideas for stylish ways in which to decorate and style your shed or other garden building? You've come to the right place. I have so many gorgeous garden retreats to share with you in *Shed Style*, from classic potting sheds (above) and shady verandas to modern garden studios and picturesque huts surrounded with pretty planting (opposite).

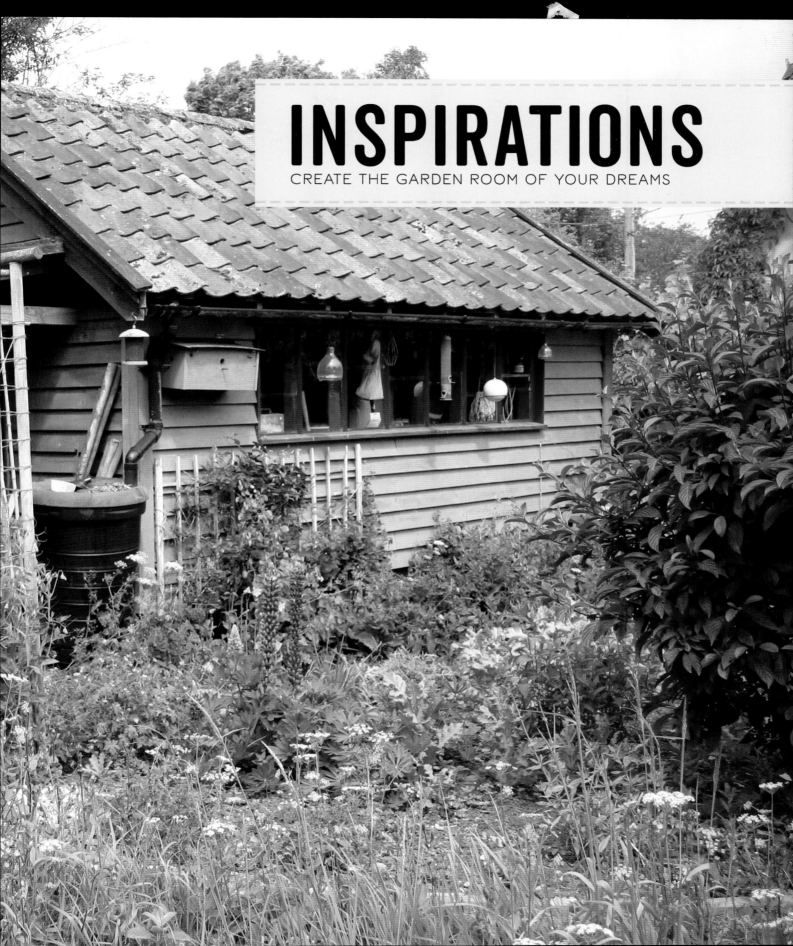

INSPIRATIONS

CREATE THE GARDEN ROOM OF YOUR DREAMS

CHOOSE YOUR
PURPOSE

Transform an existing garden building
into a versatile work or social space.

Do you dream of having a place where your creativity can flourish alongside your flowers, where you are able to connect with the great outdoors yet enjoy a sense of sanctuary? If so, take a look outside – any existing garden building can be transformed into a place to work or play. Alternatively, an underused square of lawn could be home to a newly built shed, greenhouse or garden studio.

All manner of garden buildings can be turned into a hideaway – even a humble wooden shed has the potential to become a writer's cabin or yoga studio. A greenhouse will appeal to keen gardeners, while a cosy little shepherd's hut can work as overflow guest accommodation.

I mainly use our shed as a good old-fashioned potting shed. I am very happy tinkering around in here drying flowers, repotting plants and storing seeds and bulbs. But I also enjoy styling up the space and photographing the results. You too can carve out a place to indulge in your passions and pleasures in any garden building, be it small or large.

SOW. RELAX. STYLE. REPEAT.
Keen gardeners will want to use their shed for traditional garden jobs (top left and opposite),
but if you don't have green fingers, you could use it as a place to escape and zone out (top right).
Wire suspended across a window and metal bulldog clips create a display area for a collection
of entomological prints (below left). A large greenhouse is the perfect setting for alfresco dining.
Use flowers cut from the garden to create a striking centrepiece (below right).

GREEN-FINGERED

Use your shed or greenhouse to sow, grow and enjoy all things botanical.

The original function of sheds and greenhouses was for gardening jobs. Large gardens required a garden building for numerous horticultural tasks, with greenhouses being used to grow tender plants and to speed up germination of seedlings, among other things. Keen gardeners still use sheds and greenhouses for these purposes, as well as somewhere to store gardening tools and equipment.

Although many of us now use garden buildings as extra living space, others still want to devote such structures to gardening. It's a well-loved pastime for many, and if you consider yourself to have a green thumb, you may already have what's needed to kit out a traditional shed or greenhouse. If you are new to gardening or have only recently moved to a home with a garden complete with shed, you may feel unsure where to start. To inspire your garden vision, attach images of your dream garden ripped from garden magazines to the internal walls of your shed – this will be the beginning of the botanical setting of your dreams. Then deck out your shed or garden room with some of the basics that you will need going forward. These include open shelving, a practical workbench, plant pots, labels, storage tubs and baskets. Fit hooks or racks

to keep your tools neat and organized. A functional, well-ordered shed will inspire you – if it's all set up right, you will be able to dip in and out when you have the time. Do you dream of a very traditional potting shed? Stock your space with 'shedware' (my term for shed accessories) such as balls of string, seed trays, vintage botanical prints, framed mirrors and second-hand storage drawers for storing seed packets. Some of these items can be sourced from your local garden centre, but do look out for plastic-free options when buying new, and source second-hand pieces from vintage shops specializing in gardenalia for a unique look.

HOW DOES YOUR GARDEN GROW?

I loved visiting the garden of Dorthe Kvist, a Danish garden designer. Her greenhouse features a vine scrambling across the roof and juicy peaches growing under glass (opposite below left). Cardboard boxes can be recycled as planters in the early stages of growing beans (opposite below right). Use string instead of plastic ties and terracotta pots when potting on seedlings (this page).

IN THE MOMENT
A wall painted in Railings by Farrow & Ball works with natural wooden floorboards to create a zen space ideal for yoga, meditation or Pilates (opposite). In a work area, display items that will help spark your creativity (this page).

CREATIVE & MINDFUL

Design a restful environment that's perfect for work or relaxation.

Wouldn't it be wonderful to walk into a space and immediately feel motivated, uplifted and calm? Well, a garden retreat can offer a welcome respite from the constant stresses of everyday life.

Creativity is not a state of mind you can plan as such, but having a dedicated space surrounded by items, pictures and colours that inspire you can only encourage a creative mindset. Set the scene with a workbench or desk – even an old table and a comfy chair will work well. Get imaginative with your walls – a classic moodboard made from magazine tear sheets, fabric swatches and favourite photos is a great starting point. Stick bits and pieces directly onto the walls using tape or pins, or make a separate board that can be propped up on your desk.

Perhaps you like to set aside time to practice yoga or meditation and crave a tranquil, relaxing place to participate? If so, consider turning a shed, outhouse or greenhouse into a mini studio. You'll need to clear a floor space that's big enough to roll out a yoga mat or two, then add a small table for scented candles and healthy refreshments such as water infused with herbs from the garden. Never leave lit candles unattended.

RELAXING & ENTERTAINING

Unwind, style your space and serve up a feast.

For me, the ultimate setting for a sit-down meal is the interior of a lushly stocked greenhouse. Greenhouses have an unmistakable charm that is difficult to replicate in a regular dining room. I have been lucky enough to visit some gorgeous greenhouse restaurants. Rosendals Trädgård in Stockholm, Sweden, is one of my favourite places, where three glorious vintage glasshouses are used as a café, shop and event space. On a recent family holiday to Italy, we ate at O'Parrucchiano in Sorrento – a restaurant with a greenhouse overlooking a lemon grove, plus the Italian cuisine was delicious…take me back!

To style a setting for entertaining, a certain amount of space is required, so perhaps it's time to declutter? The prospect of a lovely garden dining room will spur you on to clear out old plant pots (these can often be recycled at a local garden centre), rusty tools or other junk. Once you have made space, utilize a table that you already own. If it's old and has seen better days, that's ok – chipped paint or worn wood will add to the rustic effect. Mismatched chairs work well – wooden kitchen chairs interspersed with metal garden chairs – or two long benches are a practical way to seat multiple visitors. Now you need to prettify the space. Do this by adding cushions (and a linen tablecloth if the table has seen better days). The final decorative touches are flowers, plants or foliage. Cut whatever is abundant in the garden at the moment. Last but not least, add a scattering of tall candles and tea lights to illuminate the table as night falls.

MEET ME IN THE GARDEN
Squeeze a table into the widest space inside your shed, greenhouse or garden room (left and opposite). Round tables often work best, as you can fit in more seats. For an easy-going afternoon gathering, style up an old wooden bench or bamboo garden chairs with comfy floral-print cushions (above left). No space inside? Use your shed as a backdrop for an informal outdoor cook-up; a selection of log stumps set around a central stove make a sociable spot to hang out (above).

STYLE TIP

Reflect the garden with a well-placed mirror, which will also bounce light around your space. Colour jumps out against a dark backdrop; the internal wall in this Alitex greenhouse has been painted in Graphite Grey by M&L Paints, with the mirror frame painted to match. Bring summer colour to the table with freshly cut blooms in recycled bottles and charity/thrift shop cut-glass vases.

CHOOSE YOUR
STYLE

Take your pick from botanical, vintage, industrial, bohemian, recycled and rustic trends.

The fun thing about a small space is it can be easily changed, and a garden haven can become a place to experiment with different looks and styles – great news if you're like me and don't want to settle on one scheme. On the following pages, I explore several different styles, all of which can be intermixed with each other and work nicely within a garden setting, whatever the size.

As a starting point, take your cue from the materials of your garden building when it comes to making decorative choices. A shed constructed from rustic wood with windows salvaged from an old factory would be a perfect fit with industrial-style decor, for example. A new-build cabin or pod offers more of a blank canvas, and this is where accessories play a starring role. Add some character with a few well-chosen vintage pieces to give the interior a timeless feel. Just as you decorate and style your home with homeware accessories, your garden retreat will always benefit from some appropriate and thoughtfully chosen 'shedware'.

BLEND THE LOOK

My top tip for styling sheds and other garden buildings is to work with what you have, referencing the materials your structure is made from and including decorative pieces you already own (this page). This wood-framed greenhouse has been styled with vintage galvanized metal gardenalia, rustic wooden crates and a table constructed out of recycled wood (opposite). The concrete floor gives a nod to industrial styling, and the scheme is brought together with the addition of various plants.

BOTANICAL

Use a garden dwelling to grow, display and enjoy plants.

In a world of technology, smart phones and never-ending deadlines, tending to plants has become a relaxing pastime, a way to escape into nature. Not only that, but thanks to social media plants have become a must-have accessory for our homes and gardens. Plants make us feel good, connect us to the earth, improve air quality and feed us, so it's no wonder they are trending. Creating a potting shed or garden work area to indulge in a botanical hobby is a great idea. If you're sowing seeds, potting on or taking cuttings, a practical workbench is a necessity. If it's exotic houseplants that float your boat, create a mini botanical garden in a light room, use hanging planters to add interest to a corner or arrange pot plants on a windowsill.

CHOOSE THIS STYLE IF:

✳ *#allthingsbotanical is your favourite hashtag.*

✳ *Plant-filled spaces give you that 'at home' feeling.*

✳ *Propagating and tending to fast-growing seedlings makes you feel happy.*

✳ *Your houseplant collection is spiralling and you need more space to display your succulents.*

HUB AND HAVEN

My potting shed is a little botanical hub situated at the bottom of our garden. It's the place where I sow seeds, arrange cut flowers and escape for some peace and quiet. We inherited this old shed when my husband Dave and I bought our house a few years ago. It needed a new roof and a door, but luckily Dave is a DIY expert and soon got to work. I love having this little space to indulge in the pure pleasure of growing and gardening.

VINTAGE

Get a romantic, whimsical look with time-worn second-hand pieces.

For vintage-style garden rooms, look for muted tones, faded floral prints and items with a rich patina to create an interior with romantic charm. I'm a great fan of old French metal garden furniture, and you can source slatted folding chairs and metal tables from flea markets and vintage fairs; they are a good investment, as you can use them inside or out. Modern equivalents in pastel shades are also available. When it comes to textiles, washed linens make chic cushion covers and are durable outside. When it comes to sourcing vintage wares, buy direct from vintage traders. That way, you can ask for the provenance of the piece to determine whether it's a genuine item. The vintage style can also include inherited items, allowing family pieces to shine. It's nice to include such treasures in spaces you love to spend time in.

BLOOMING LOVELY

Romantic florals are the ideal addition to any vintage scheme. Style your space with potted perennials like this foxglove (opposite above) or tiny specimens snipped from the garden (opposite below left). You can even pin up floral prints (right). Utilitarian enamelware is a perfect fit for this look (opposite below right). Look for vintage garden furniture at fairs and flea markets (above right). Old terracotta pots strike the right note (above left).

INDUSTRIAL

Create a rougher edge with utilitarian items, enamel lighting and distressed finishes.

The industrial style takes its cue from old factories and warehouses converted to lofts and trendy bars, and is particularly well suited to garden workshops and converted garages. The key features of the look include exposed brick, concrete flooring, metal-framed windows, enamel accessories and suspended naked bulb lighting. To get the look, clad walls in corrugated metal sheeting or allow a scuffed plaster finish to become a feature. Seek out freestanding furniture that can easily be moved; metal racks on wheels are a good option, and wire baskets are ideal for holding smaller bits and pieces. If metal pieces have a light coating of rust, that's a bonus, as it adds another layer to the look. To finish, introduce colour in the form of plants and accessories – natural greens blend in beautifully, while small pops of red and orange will enliven the scene.

CHOOSE THIS STYLE IF:

✳ *An rugged urban look is your style goal.*
✳ *Metal greys, blacks and browns are your colours.*
✳ *Vintage metal is your go-to material for shedware accessories.*
✳ *Your garden building has been converted from a workshop or garage.*

TOUGHEN UP

The industrial look has a rough and ready charm. It draws inspiration from old factories and industrial premises, so embraces exposed beans or ceiling struts (opposite below left), rusting metal surfaces and scuffed or pitted walls (this page). Luckily, flowers and greenery look great against these battered finishes. When it comes to choosing decorative accessories, stick to old rusting metal and raw wood, and adhere to a neutral colour palette (opposite below right and above left).

BOHEMIAN

A nomad-inspired scheme for would-be globetrotters.

Bohemian style celebrates an eclectic, free-spirited look with layered patterns and a multicultural vibe. For me, it conjures up images of hand-painted Romany caravans, the souks of Morocco and block-printed Indian fabrics. To create a bohemian vibe, I've mixed patterned textiles with shades of rust, dusky pink and earthy tones, and combined them with natural and sustainable materials such as bamboo, woven baskets and artisan clay vases. The overall effect mixes global influences with an on-trend simplicity courtesy of Scandinavian design. Bohemian-style furniture celebrates retro and second-hand pieces – 1970s bamboo peacock chairs or macramé swing seats. Natural elements are a great fit; look for tree-stump stools and use branches and dried leaves as decorations, creating an inside/outside feel.

CHOOSE THIS STYLE IF:

✳ *You like to mix up varying global styles.*

✳ *Earthy tones make you feel calm and grounded.*

✳ *You crave a chilled, laid-back space.*

✳ *A matchy-matchy approach is not your vibe.*

✳ *You need somewhere to display items brought back from your travels.*

GLOBAL INSPIRATION

Nothing could be more bohemian than whiling away a few hours on low-level seating or a daybed styled with cushions and throws on a warm sunny day (opposite right and this page). To get the look, use items you have collected on your travels – bamboo furniture, printed Indian textiles and Moroccan wedding blankets. Lighting is best when it's kept soft and romantic; opt for a simple string of fairy lights, candle lanterns or decorative paper shades that cast a warm glow (opposite page and above). For the perfect accessories, explore Danish brands such as bungalow.dk and Madam Stoltz.

RECYCLED

Get creative with salvaged materials for recycled chic.

In this day and age, when we are focused on preserving natural resources, opting to recycle existing materials and accessories is a wise choice. Not only does the use of salvaged materials keep a project on budget, but it's a very desirable look. If you have the skills, building your own shed from reclaimed materials is the sustainable way to go, and the result will be unique. You could customize an existing or new shed by cladding exterior walls with corrugated metal, getting creative with salvaged roofing materials or styling the interior with recycled furniture. Another option is to seek out a recycled dwelling made by artisan makers, such as the little tin shed shown opposite, which was made by The Old Yard in Shropshire, UK.

CHOOSE THIS STYLE IF:

✷ *You can't walk past a junk shop or salvage yard without stopping to have a good old browse.*

✷ *A garden dwelling with eco credentials is your goal.*

✷ *One-of-a-kind spaces draw you in.*

✷ *DIY doesn't faze you in the slightest.*

✷ *Old things spark your imagination.*

SECOND TIME AROUND

Recycled materials and salvaged pieces bring warmth and interest to a garden, and you can guarantee that no-one else will have exactly the same as you (right and opposite page). It may look as if it's been here forever, but this shed in Debbie Smail's garden was made from recycled materials by The Old Yard in Shropshire (above right). The structure is corrugated tin, while the salvaged window has a narrow sill that's the right width for a display of garden blooms (above left).

RUSTIC

Create a *hygge* hideaway with modern rustic details.

Rustic style is rugged, raw and embraces natural beauty. It calls for genuine, unpolished textures and an unpretentious, organic mood. Creative husband and wife team Atlanta Bartlett and Dave Coote lined the walls of their rustic cabin (shown opposite) in rough-cut timber logs and patinated corrugated steel panels. A simple kitchenette sits against one wall to create a look that combines the industrial trend with a romantic woodland hideaway.

Rustic styling can bring a new flat-pack shed personality and atmosphere. Accessorize with enamelled storm lanterns and handmade details carved from wood. Textiles strike a cosy note – look for vintage Welsh blankets and linen grain-sack cushions.

CHOOSE THIS STYLE IF:

✳ *You dream about running away to an Alpine chalet or a remote lakeside cabin.*

✳ *Earthy natural hues and natural or distressed textures are your thing.*

✳ *A cosy 'away-from-it-all' feel is required.*

✳ *You already have an old garden building with an aged patina.*

RUSTIC ESCAPES

Atlanta Bartlett and Dave Coote's rustic cabin is lined with split logs and sheets of salvaged corrugated metal (this page). Glass jars have been upcycled into hanging lanterns with wire and hung from hooks against a rugged wood wall (opposite above right) A DIY shelf fashioned from an old plank of wood tied with string at each end and suspended from the roof of a greenhouse or shed (opposite) makes a useful and decorative display for pots of pink pelargoniums. If you're lucky enough to have an old wooden garden structure, rustic styling is a perfect fit (opposite below).

DECORATIVE
ELEMENTS

All the essentials for styling your shed, cabin or other garden building.

Once you've decided on the function of your garden building and the style that suits you best, it's time to get down to the nitty-gritty and focus on the key decorative elements of your shed, greenhouse, cabin or whatever. In this section of the book, I aim to help you choose the right elements for your garden building.

The surfaces will set the tone for a decorative mood. Review the previous pages and think about the look you want to create. Rusty corrugated iron for an industrial vibe, or unpainted wood to provide a backdrop for your botanical treasures? This will guide you to make the right choices.

Your furniture selection will depend on what you plan to do in your garden retreat. If you're going to be reading and relaxing, look for a comfy armchair, while a creative workspace will require a desk and chair. And finally, there's the fun part – the decorative finishing touches. Lighting, soft furnishings and accessories are key in creating the right mood.

ALL IN THE DETAIL

Pretty decorative details make a garden feel loved. An assortment of glass bottles has been painted in M&L exterior paint and arranged on a painted metal tray (top left). A rustic dovecote doubles as support for a climbing honeysuckle (top right). Old wooden railings complete with their original peeling paint have been used to add a decorative element to a veranda (above left). A simple wooden peg rail is the ideal spot to hang old metal storm lanterns (above right).

MATERIALS & TEXTURES

An artful blend of materials and textiles will bring a garden hub to life.

Your choice of building or decorating materials will have a huge impact on the overall style of your garden room. Layering several different textures adds interest and appealing variety to any interior.

First and foremost, invest in practical, hard-working materials that will offer insulation and warmth. There's no point having a beautiful cabin or summer house that isn't watertight. Secondly, take your cue from your preferred decorative style. If you like all things natural, opt for natural textures in the shape of woven palm leaf hangings, bamboo screening and jute rugs. Display plants in baskets

and make arrangements of dried flowers. For a nod to the recycled or industrial look, opt for corrugated metal sheets or old wood to clad walls both inside and out. Gather your collection of metal gardenalia and combine it with weathered wooden crates. A vintage look calls for something softer. Give walls a lick of paint in a muted shade and hang cotton or linen curtains at the window. Linen cushions and floral prints will strike the right note. Bohemian textures are richer and ethnic prints have a role to play. Velvet cushions, block-printed cottons and bamboo furniture are the right textures for this look.

TEXTURAL APPEAL

Recycled wooden doors lead to this ingenious outdoor cabin-style shower, while corrugated metal sheeting bolted onto a solid wooden frame gives an industrial-style backdrop to a sheltered seating area (opposite page). Unattractive walls of modern brick are easily concealed behind reclaimed wooden cladding or inexpensive reed screening (this page). Grimy concrete floors can be pressure-washed, then painted with floor paint and softened with a jute or all-weather rug (below right). Rustic accessories are the perfect finishing touch (right), and plants in terracotta pots bring any space to life (below left).

PERFECTLY PATINATED
We often talk about the charm
of a patina in the styling and
interiors world – it's simply
a faded, rusted, tarnished or
worn surface that has become
a decorative feature in itself.
Reusing old metal or wood that
has developed a pleasing patina
will benefit the environment and
improve your shed's visual appeal.

GET THE RIGHT FINISH
For a robust, weather-resistant finish, choose a tough yet breathable exterior paint that's designed for use on a variety of different surfaces, including brick, wood and metal (this page and opposite).

PAINTED SURFACES

Use paint to transform a garden retreat and protect it from the elements.

Personally, I'm drawn to neutral colours for exterior structures, garden buildings and outdoor furniture, as I want these man-made objects to blend into the garden, giving the plants a chance to shine. My preferred shades are natural earthy tones such as black, brown, rust, honey and green.

Colour is a personal choice, however, and maybe you're drawn to burnt orange, inky blue or vibrant pink...the choice is yours. The best thing about a small garden building is that it won't take much time or paint to give it a new look (although if you are painting over a dark colour you'll need to give your shed an undercoat of white paint first). A bold, bright colour on the interior walls of a garden building could limit its styling potential, so I'd recommend a neutral backdrop if you want to make the most of the space. Super-bright 'out there' colours date fast and are best used to highlight smaller areas such as window frames or doors. By the way, painting wood and metal structures with the appropriate specialist outdoor paint will protect the material and prolong the life of your shed.

SOURCE SECOND-HAND
This large greenhouse is home to an array of covetable vintage furniture (opposite). A retro bamboo sofa and chair can be carried outside when the weather allows (above). Folding chairs are versatile – use them to seat guests or as side tables (left).

FURNITURE

Furnish your garden room with versatile pieces.

Specific garden furniture is an obvious choice and you can find attractive pieces made from weatherproof materials in large stores and garden centres. However, if your shed or studio is watertight, then indoor items can be used outside – a daybed or old leather armchair, perhaps. Look for items that fit the decorative style you've chosen. A wicker chair is perfect for a bohemian space, for example, whereas an old metal workbench will suit an industrial theme.

Select practical pieces that will serve a purpose in your garden dwelling – don't get into the habit of banishing items to outdoor rooms when you no longer have use

for them inside! If your outdoor space is going to be multifunctional, opt for pieces that are easy to move. Bamboo or rattan furniture is lightweight, so it's an excellent choice. A simple tabletop on trestle legs can be used as a surface to work or craft on and is easily dismantled and tucked away when necessary. And you can never have too much storage. Open shelving will allow you to showcase favourite items, while closed storage is best for less attractive or practical pieces.

When it's time to relax, make a garden bench inviting with a seat mattress and cushions or, if you have the space, upholstered armchairs and daybeds are winners.

SUPER COMFY

I like to dress my garden bench with an assortment of cushions when the sun shines. This selection includes a block-printed leaf design by Walter G, a hand-drawn dragonfly cushion by Delia Rose Illustration and a ruffled black linen cushion from Also Home (opposite). On stylist Dee Campling's veranda, an old leather sofa has been cosied up with a mix of vintage and patterned cushions (above). For similar, try Etsy. A rustic-themed wooden cabin is home to these snug bunks dressed in vintage-style floral duvets (left).

SOFT FURNISHINGS

Cosy handmade cushions and throws provide a homely feel.

Soft furnishings are one of my go-to styling props, as they have the power to instantly create the right mood or transform the feel of a space. When it comes to choosing textiles, I steer towards natural materials such as linen, hemp or organic cotton. I also like decorative elements such as tassels, fringing and embroidery, and mix in handmade screen-printed designs, which I source via Etsy. Nowadays there are special outdoor fabrics designed to withstand the weather, but I'm all for making use of what I already have. I'm a firm believer that any textiles that can be washed in the machine can be used outside and I'm not averse to taking eiderdowns off my beds and using them to comfy up our garden bench – after all, they can be always be hand washed or dry cleaned.

Botanical and entomological prints featuring bees, leaves, florals or fruits are all particularly fitting for a garden dwelling. If you prefer a nostalgic, rustic vibe, vintage floral-printed linens in muted tones will create the right effect. For a cosy cabin for winter days, knitted and woollen blankets are essential, along with chunky rugs that are soft and warm underfoot.

Another way to introduce textiles is in the form of furniture. Armchairs with loose covers/slipcovers are an excellent idea, as you can whip them off whenever they are in need of a wash. Fabrics can also be used as decorative and insulating wall coverings – tack up a flatweave rug to keep out cold draughts, or hang your favourite piece of fabric on the wall instead of art.

LIGHTING

When the sun goes down, turn to clever lighting ideas.

For daytime tasks in your shed, cabin or garden pod you are likely to need some form of task lighting. If you are connected to an electricity supply, opt for an anglepoise-style desk lamp to illuminate crafting, office work or reading. If not, leave the door open, keep the windows uncovered and let the natural light stream in.

If you're intending to entertain after dark, atmospheric lighting will add ambience to any gathering. For small spaces, choose simple, space-saving lighting such as battery-operated or solar-powered string lights. Neat metal or enamelled pendant shades or wall lights are also good options. A larger space with a higher ceiling capacity allows for some statement lighting – perhaps a cluster of glass pendants, a chandelier or oversized rattan lampshades. No power? No problem. There are so many solar-powered lights on the market nowadays – just remember to fit the solar panel in a sunny spot and choose options with a warm tone rather than anything too cold and blue. Candles are an immediate and cost-effective way to add light. Use glass lanterns for pillar candles and recycled food jars for tea lights, or track down a candle candelabra.

ILLUMINATING WAYS
A string of solar-powered lights illuminate the way to a garden cabin (above left) Green enamel pendant lights and plenty of candles light up a lean-to greenhouse converted into an outdoor dining spot (above right). Tea lights, candles, candelabras and glass pendants are all great sources of light for a garden building (opposite).

THE DARK SIDE

Black paint works brilliantly in the garden, as it fades into the background. Here, shelves painted the same colour as the wall provide the perfect backdrop for plants, pots and other gardenalia (above right). The exterior wall of this cabin is clad with wood stained black for a Scandi look, with a vintage dovecote hanging alongside old birdcages (top left). Old ladders are both decorative and functional, and if the treads are wide enough, you can arrange plants on them too (above).

SEASONAL CHANGES
A black-painted shelf unit on the side of a shed is home to a seasonal display of winter pansies (above). My treasured rustic crate is my favourite spot for seasonal displays. It moves into the shed in the winter months to prevent the wood from rotting (right).

DISPLAY IDEAS

Take time to show off your treasured posessions.

As a stylist, creating displays is my forte, and you can also create Instagram-worthy areas in your garden with a couple of my styling tips and tricks. Once I've created something I like, I keep it in place, then swap the ingredients to suit different seasons and events or whenever inspiration strikes. To start, you'll need a surface such as open shelving, a wall unit, a bench or a small folding or trestle table. Gather up a few items you have lurking around your garden or shed. Vintage-style metal storm lanterns, old terracotta pots, birdhouses, glass or ceramic vases, urns, tiles, watering cans and potted plants are all good options. Now arrange them. The secret is combining items of different heights, as this creates visual interest. If your pieces are a similar height, use old bricks, upturned crates and log stumps to raise some of them. If you want to create a 'gallery wall', look for vintage signs, wall-mounted planters, birdhouses or old mirrors. As with pictures, it's a wise idea to arrange them on the ground first to decide on positioning before screwing or nailing holes in the wall.

SHEDS

EVERY GARDEN NEEDS A SHED

AT THE BOTTOM OF THE GARDEN
Plants, foliage and flowers soften man-made structures and help integrate them into the garden (left and opposite). An array of seasonal plants in terracotta pots (no plastic, please!) will add charm to even the most basic shed (above).

THE NOT-SO-HUMBLE SHED

Sheds are versatile little structures - what will you use yours for?

You may be of the mindset that the garden shed is a humble wooden structure hidden away at the bottom of your plot and used to store tools and bags of compost. I'm hoping *Shed Style* will turn any such preconceptions on their head and help you to see these hard-working garden buildings in a completely new light. Your shed can be your own little palace at the end of the garden, a space where you can participate in a multitude of activities and decorated with the interior of your dreams. Think of it as a mini hideaway where you can escape the chores and stresses of everyday life.

Perhaps you already own a shed but are not sure how best to use it? Decide on the pastime of your choice – crafting, meditating, reading, potting up plants – then set about creating the ideal space for this hobby. Of course, there are practical limitations to consider. Your structure will need to be watertight and you may need power, which will involve a visit from an electrician. There are also solar power panels designed for sheds. If you need to share the space with tools and those compost bags, get clever with storage. Are there any nifty ways to divide it? Even a simple muslin/cheesecloth curtain will do the trick.

One of the best ways to give your shed a charming first impression is with a spruce exterior. Make it look attractive by arranging pots and lanterns around the door. Fit blinds or pin up fabric to screen the windows inside. I really like the Field Study printed fabric by Jacqueline Milton, which features a botanical design of foraged finds and bugs, bees and butterflies.

You can also get creative with the route from your house to the shed. Choose stepping stones for a fun approach, reuse old bricks to make a decorative path or simply leave your lawn to grow long and wild and full of flowers, then mow a path through it.

ŠTEPENIE DO BOKU

SALVAGED STYLE
Reclaimed furniture works well in a rustic wooden shed (this page). Your local reclamation yard is the place to rummage for old trestles, tables, benches, folding chairs and much more. There may also be some attractive gardenalia, allowing you to continue the theme elsewhere on your plot.

A CUTTING GARDEN

Use your plot to grow seasonal flowers for your home.

PLASTIC FREE
Wherever possible, I try not to use any plastic in the garden. I'm a huge fan of vintage garden tools like the wooden spade shown here, which has been well-used yet still has many years of service ahead (above left). Baskets are ideal for harvesting home-grown produce and cut flowers (above centre), and you can use wooden labels to mark where seeds are sown (above right).

Of course, you don't actually need a shed in order to grow your own flowers – just a patch of weed-free ground plus some seeds, bulbs or tubers. Oh, and a little time and patience...and to have the weather on your side. However, a dedicated space for storing gardening equipment, seeds and other tools will make any such project much easier.

A shed allows you to indulge in your hobby on wet-weather days, providing protection from the elements and somewhere to hide out when the storms roll in. It's a dedicated spot where you can sort and dry seeds and store bulbs between growing seasons. Fit shelving in the interior and use old tin boxes to stash seeds – remember to label the packets before you put them away.

The cute wooden shed shown opposite is owned by Lou Grace, a gardener with a garden and two allotments that she tends to with great care and dedication. Inside, there's a broad, built-in potting bench where Lou gathers her freshly picked blooms and arranges them. She had plenty of practical shelving fitted and painted the interior white, creating a fresh, bright backdrop that works well when Lou is creating her colourful floral arrangements. You can create a similar cutting garden shed by customizing a flatpack shed from the DIY store or garden centre. Even the humblest structure can be tailored to meet your needs – start by installing a workbench and creating some storage space before tackling the decoration, both inside and out.

PRETTY PICKINGS

A generous workbench is the ideal place to allow
cut blooms to have a long drink before making
up arrangements (above and opposite above right).
Another workbench job is seed collecting. Plants
produce flowers to make seeds, creating more plants
and flowers in turn. You can collect seeds from your
own garden, dry them, store them in paper envelopes
and sow them the following year. I like to craft my
own pretty packets from botanical-themed gift wrap
to hold the seeds until they are ready to sow. They
make great presents too (right).

CUT AND DRIED

If you already have a flower patch, consider growing varieties that can be used in dried arrangements. Most garden flowers can be air-dried, including lavender and roses, and a dark, dry shed is the ideal place to do it. Hang them upside down suspended from a nail, hook or coat hanger. Flowers with sturdy stems such as alliums and hydrangeas can dry out in large (empty) flower buckets (above). Lou's husband Russ uses metal to make garden decorations, frames and plant supports. He built this structure on their allotment for Lou's sweet peas and beans (right).

A PAINTED SUMMER
GARDEN SHED

A lick of paint will make even the humblest garden shed as pretty as a picture.

This quaint painted shed is owned by my fellow author and stylist Jane Cumberbatch. I have had the pleasure of styling it for various photoshoots over the years, and I'm delighted to be able to include it in this book.

The shed's exterior is painted with Little Greene exterior eggshell in Cupboard Green, while the interior is zesty Kitchen Green, with the trim painted to match the outside. Natural wood always works well with painted surfaces, so outside Jane's shed I erected a makeshift table made from a weathered wooden door on two sturdy trestles and gathered together a collection of plants for a decorative display. If you have a piece of new wooden garden furniture but prefer an aged effect, leave it outside in all weathers and it will soon develop the desired patina.

Inside the shed, a vintage wooden apple rack sourced from a flea market looks striking set against the painted walls and inspired me to create another display combining seasonal plants with vintage gardenalia and terracotta pots (overleaf).

Jane has a very pretty country-style garden with borders that explode into colour from early spring. The area in front of the shed is laid to lawn, making it a good spot to position a dining table – somewhere to enjoy a relaxed lunch on a sunny day. The table was originally painted to match the shed but has since faded, creating an appealing distressed finish. The slatted wood and metal chairs (a lucky find at a flea market) are typical of Jane's timeless style.

CHOICE COLOURS
Before painting your shed, give some thought to selecting the right colour – one that matches your chosen decorative style and works well with any furniture you already have. Paint swatches on the exterior to help you choose and wait till the paint has dried completely before making your decision. My preferred colours for exteriors are greens, black and dark earthy browns, as well as off-white (but not cream).

TAKE A MOMENT
With large windows at the front and a glass panel in the door, the interior of Jane's shed is bright and airy (this page). The canvas director's chair offers a sweet spot to pause, catch up on garden reading and take a breath before the next task (below).

THE WILD FLOWERS OF BRITAIN AND NORTHERN EUROPE

TABLETOP DISPLAY

As a stylist and a garden lover, I'm at my most contented when putting together decorative arrangements like this one (opposite). It makes me happy to see a seasonal array of plants and it's so easy to change it with the seasons. If you've not tried something like this before, gather together a selection of items you already have. Glass bottles, for example, can be used as vases, while ugly plastic plant pots can be disguised by popping them into a basket.

SELINA'S OWN
POTTING SHED

Welcome to my beloved garden shed, where the idea for this book began.

My shed is a little botanical hub situated at the bottom of our garden. It's somewhere I visit to sow seeds, pot on seedlings, create decorative displays and generally escape the mundane. My husband Dave and I inherited this shed in a very run-down state when we bought our house. It had clearly been neglected for years; the door was missing and the roof was caving in. Luckily, Dave is a super DIY-er, with skills that have impressed me since the day we first met, and he set aside a long weekend to construct a new door and roof. When we moved in, we had visions of building a summer house on this plot, so these fixes were intended as a temporary measure. However, five years on, we are still plotting and planning that summer house (it will happen one day!).

In the meantime, I love our little shed. As soon as Dave fixed it up, I decided to stain it black, inspired by cabins and summer houses seen

on my travels to Denmark and Sweden. Inside, I kept the walls just as I found them – the wood has a lovely rustic quality that only the passage of time can create. The previous owner had left behind a big wooden cabinet (the base unit of an old dresser/hutch, we suspect) and I use this as my potting bench. At the front of the shed, under the window, I either place a small metal table or a wooden plant stand, also stained black, and use these as the bases for seasonal displays. They also double up as handy storage for all the odd little bits and pieces that I use as props in my styling work.

PAINT IT BLACK
Inspired by trips to Scandinavia, I decided to paint our shed black using a Ronseal wood stain called Tudor Black Oak (opposite and left). It's a great foil for greenery and brightly coloured flowers. The wood is old, so it does need to be re-stained every spring to keep the exterior a deep, rich black. I keep my straw gardening hat hanging from a nail inside the shed door, close at hand for sunny days (above).

SHED CHIC

When it comes to styling our shed, I like to mix flowering plants with botanical prints and drawings and vintage gardenalia (this page and opposite). Opposite the door, a little nook is home to a garden workstation (below) constructed from IKEA metal trestles and two scaffold planks cut to size. It's great to have a workspace outside when the weather's good. I also use it as a place to harden off seedlings before planting them out.

GREENHOUSES

PRACTICAL AND BEAUTIFUL SPACES FOR THE GARDEN

THE FEEL-GOOD FACTOR
A Victorian-style greenhouse such as this one will bring the charm of yesteryear to any garden (left). At The Norrmans B&B in Denmark, this charming structure is part-shed, part-greenhouse – the best of both worlds (above and opposite).

GREENHOUSE GOALS

Create the ultimate retreat under glass where you and your plants can flourish.

For me, glasshouses (or hothouses, as they are also known) have it all – warmth from the sun, views of the garden and plenty of nostalgic charm. I may have rose-tinted views, I admit, as I have such wonderful memories of my parents' greenhouse when I was a child.

When I visit gardens, it's often the garden structures that catch my attention. Unloved, forgotten greenhouses have a romantic allure for me, and I like to daydream about bringing them back to their former glory – think of the glorious parties you could throw inside a roomy glasshouse! While a grand greenhouse would be my garden dream, you need a large budget to maintain

one, especially as jobs such as replacing broken glass and repairing cracked windows are common. A small greenhouse is a much more realistic proposition!

A greenhouse interior needs careful planning. Shelves are essential – somewhere to store pots, seed trays, tools and plant labels. They also provide a place to style gardening items and create decorative vignettes. If there's space, bring in a table and a couple of garden chairs to make a pretty seating area, or introduce a bench that can be cosied up with a seat mattress and cushions. If that isn't possible, use your greenhouse to store folding furniture that can be put up outside on warm days.

PRETTY PANES
The greenhouse windows at Rosendals Trädgård in Stockholm, Sweden, are a famous feature (opposite). The in-house florist puts together a display using flowers from the gardens. Create a similar effect in your own greenhouse by hanging a couple of shelves and collecting recycled jars, pots and bud vases (this page).

STYLE TIP

For optimum greenhouse good looks, group together galvanized metal items or old terracotta pots on a nearby workbench or beside the door. A wooden or metal bench outside the greenhouse can be used to display attractive pots or left clear for a sit-down and a cup of tea on a sunny afternoon.

NATURAL ACCESSORIES

Creating a greenhouse sanctuary is all about striking the right balance between practicality and relaxation. Ideally, your greenhouse will have enough space for cultivation as well as a spot for you to chill out (above). To hit the appropriate note, seek out furniture made from natural materials such as bamboo and rattan, or rustic and painted wood. On shelves or a work table, style up little vignettes as shown here, using vintage glass bottles, aged terracotta plant pots and woven baskets and platters (right and above right).

SEASONAL STYLE

Celebrate the seasons and what nature has to offer.

If I had to choose, spring would be my favourite season for pottering around in the greenhouse. This is the time to get the space ready for the gardening year ahead, sweeping it out and giving it a tidy. At this time of year, the seedlings are growing fast and trees are laden with blossom, plus there is the delicious promise in the air of lovely long, hot summer days ahead.

Having a working greenhouse means you're in tune with the seasons, so what could be more fitting than decorative touches that celebrate the natural world? A single branch from one of those blossom trees would be beautiful poking out from an old metal watering can. Bringing in signs of the changing seasons makes your space pleasing to look at and more enjoyable to be in. Of course, I'm not suggesting you go to the trouble of making your greenhouse look lovely without posting a picture via social media, if that's your thing. I find garden inspiration via Pinterest and Instagram, and love to follow @gertrudsrum @rosendalstradgard and @familjengron. For first-hand inspiration, I head to Petersham Nurseries in Richmond, Surrey, and marvel at their ever-changing seasonal displays.

RINGING THE CHANGES
'A change is a good as a rest' is something my lovely mum says quite often. A new season brings new ideas, new plants and new ways to make the most of our gardens. Celebrate this change with an arrangement of garden cuttings, a seasonal handmade wreath or a new colour palette to reflect the current mood.

SIGNS OF SPRING

It may be too cold to sit outside, but if your greenhouse is big enough to hold a small table, transform it into a space for enjoying tea and cake with friends and family (opposite). I love to put together a seasonal display, like this one of delicate spring bulbs and blossom (this page). Pots of snowdrops sit alongside pussy willow stems in a large glass vase, with small posies of narcissi, hellebores and sarcococca (sweet box) clustered in vintage vases. I stuck botanical prints to the windows using washi tape.

A KEEN GARDENER'S
WORKSPACE

This hand-built greenhouse in a pretty Swedish garden is a romantic spot.

This wood and glass structure was built by skilled carpenter Peter Wallin especially for his wife Lena. And people say romance is dead! The couple live in the Swedish countryside and their garden lies at the edge of a forest, meaning they have lush views from their greenhouse all year round (you can follow Lena on Instagram @lenasskoghem). The building has been ingeniously designed with an apex glass roof and a salvaged stained glass window inserted into the back wall (see page 85) to allow in maximum rays. The layout enables Lena to grow crops in built-in brick raised beds, and there's also space for a couple of armchairs for when it's time to relax.

The plot naturally slopes up towards the forest and Peter has cleverly factored this into the design. Outside, a woven hazel fence separates the lawn from the gravelled area that surrounds the greenhouse. Directly in front of the door, Peter has built a selection of raised wooden beds for hardier crops such as root vegetables. Lena has given this area a welcoming feel, with a natural theme

that's in keeping with the style of their garden and the surroundings. Her treasured collection of pots, baskets and watering cans is neatly displayed both inside and out. It's a good idea to choose accessories that are both practical and match your aesthetic. Peter screwed a couple of handy hooks directly into the wall so that Lena can hang lanterns (see page 84 above right), and metal tubs and barrels have been recycled to make interesting planters at the entrance.

RAISE YOUR GAME
Laying gravel between raised beds is a good way to create clean, dry paths, and it's not too expensive either. It's advisable to put down a weed-suppressing membrane first and then layer the gravel on top, as it's always an annoying job to weed a path or patio. Bear in mind that the gravel will need topping up every five years or so.

RECYCLE AND REPURPOSE
Chucking out a tired bedside table/nightstand? Why not give it new purpose in the garden by using it to display planters and store plant pots (left)? The little drawer will come in handy for storing plant ties and labels.

BAMBOO REVIVAL
This natural material was all the rage in the 1970s and has made a huge comeback in recent years. It's hard-wearing and ages beautifully, making it ideal for outdoor furniture and a brilliant and sustainable alternative to plastic. Look out for second-hand bamboo furniture that can be given a new life (right). Lena sourced this chair from a vintage shop and has cosied it up with a padded seat cushion and draped throw.

AN AWARD-WINNING
GREENHOUSE

My 'floral party'-inspired greenhouse
at the RHS Chelsea Flower Show.

Being commissioned to style the Alitex stand at the RHS Chelsea Flower Show in London, the most prestigious horticultural show in the world, was a dream job as well as a personal career highlight for me. Alitex specializes in greenhouses and conservatories, designing and building unique spaces where plants thrive and people flourish. It's a family business and has been exhibiting at RHS Chelsea for more than 50 years.

I wanted the Alitex stand to be a talking point at the fair, so I devised a vibrant 'floral party' theme to showcase their bespoke greenhouse. The theme celebrated all things floral – very fitting for the famous flower show – and gave visitors a treat for all the senses. The generous size of the structure provided an opportunity to demonstrate a multitude of different uses for a greenhouse. The main feature was a dining table surrounded by mismatched chairs. With the assistance of Sarah Prall, I dressed it with

seasonal cut flowers in glass vases. By the door, I arranged a bamboo bench from IKEA layered with vintage eiderdowns and a mattress from Danish homeware brand bungalow.dk.

When it came to styling the greenhouse, I deliberately opted for items not typically associated with the outdoors, such as neon lighting by Love Inc., cushions, mirrors, framed artworks and fringed glass pendant lights by Rothschild & Bickers. The greenhouse even made it onto prime-time television via the BBC coverage of the show. To top it all, the stand received five stars – the highest possible accolade from the judges.

PICTURE PERFECT
Adding print, paintings and even a neon artwork to the interior of the greenhouse was all part of the 'floral party' theme (opposite). The 'Stop and Smell the Roses' print from Basil and Ford was a perfect fit, as was artwork by Jennifer Allevato, sourced via Anthropologie. I thought it would be fun to include a picture of a greenhouse inside a greenhouse and came across this sweet painting by Peggy & Kate (above).

FULL-ON FLORALS

For a blooming floral table display, I blended floral patterns using classic Chelsea Fabric by Sanderson with masses of fresh British-grown perennial plants and cut flowers such as foxgloves, delphiniums and sweet peas (left). The planting scheme in front of the greenhouse is by garden designer Jake Curley (see page 87 below and below right). For maximum wow factor, I grouped colourful plants in pots together (below left and opposite above).

PAINTED PIECES

Alitex launched a new range of exterior and garden paints from their sister brand M&L Paints at the show, so I incorporated the new colours into the styling theme. I painted vintage chairs in Plaster Pink and Burnt Orange (right and opposite right), and a watering can was given an update in Deep Mauve. All these colourful pieces pop against the Graphite Grey interior of the greenhouse.

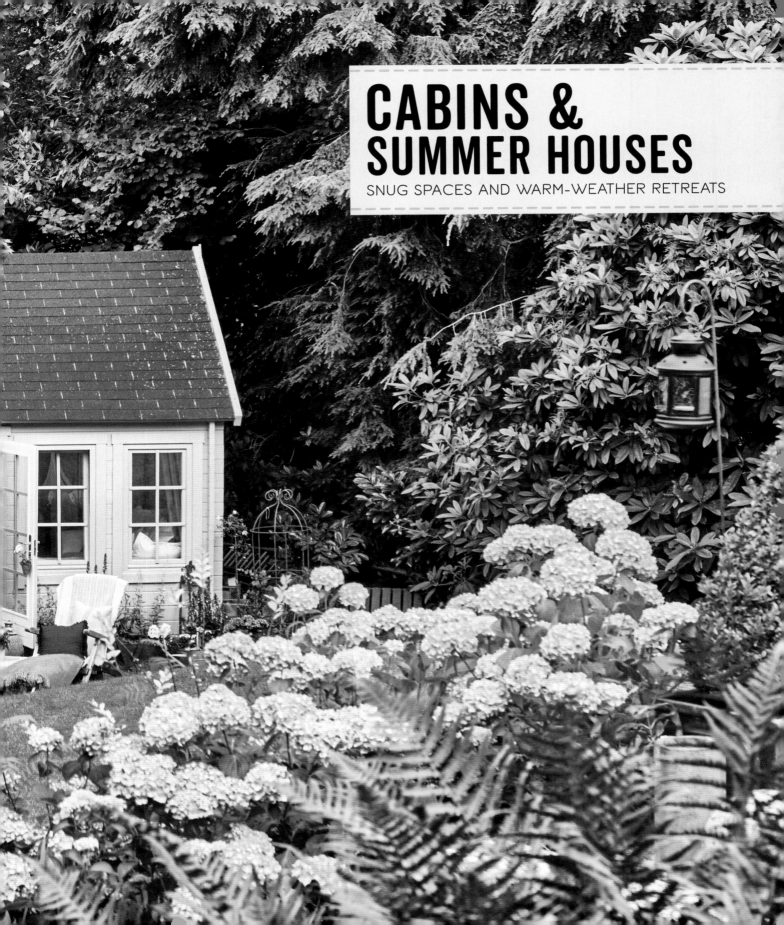

CABINS & SUMMER HOUSES
SNUG SPACES AND WARM-WEATHER RETREATS

COSY CABINS

Hunker down on winter days in your own garden room.

WARM AND WELCOMING

Weathered timber used on the exterior of this cabin and the glow from the windows make a welcoming first impression (above left). No stove or power supply to your cabin? Keep warm by wearing chunky sweaters (above centre). A rustic ladder displays cosy blankets (above right). A wood-burning stove will pump out heat during the winter months (opposite).

On a chilly winter's day, the idea of a snug cabin at the bottom of the garden is more than appealing. Traditionally made from stacked or split logs, cabins have a long history in both Europe and America, where they are associated with the first settlers. Nowadays the term is more commonly used to refer to a rustic-style wooden or wood-clad building rather than one made from roughly hewn logs. Cabins have a homely, bucolic charm and offer a sense of escape from the 'real world'.

Modern garden cabins often draw inspiration from black-stained Scandinavian summer cabins or are clad in rustic raw wood. If you envisage using your cabin during the winter months, it will require a few key elements to make it habitable. Some source of heating is a must.

If there's the budget, install a wood-burning stove for maximum Scandi *hygge* factor and make a feature out of displaying piles of logs and kindling. A power supply will allow you to plug in an electric radiator. Or for a more primitive space, gather together cushions, quilts, throws and hot water bottles, and don cosy knitted socks and sweaters to keep you warm.

Furnish a cabin with a comfy sofa or armchair covered in a mohair throw or Welsh blanket, then add an armful of cushions. Alternatively, you could create a dining area for intimate dinners lit by candlelight. A cosy cabin can offer a romantic space, a bolt-hole to hunker down with your loved ones or a place to hibernate, rest and retreat from the rest of the world.

STYLE TIP

Layered sheepskins and rugs scattered across the floor bring instant cosiness to a traditional log cabin. Kilim cushions add colour and pattern to a simple sofa, while retro-style metal wall lights provide contrast with rustic log walls. The Morsø stove creates a toasty vibe, and the windows have been left bare to allow light to flood in.

IN A DEEP DARK WOOD

Give a cabin a woodland theme with earthy tones, deep dark shades and natural elements (this page). Use natural materials to make decorations such as rustic wreaths or simple arrangements (left and above). This garden shed-cum-rustic cabin has an autumnal vibe thanks to the thick layer of leaves that covers the floor (opposite). The built-in bench has been styled with faux fur, velvet and vintage floral cushions. The neon pink touches are unexpected and add an element of fun.

ANTIQUE & VINTAGE

A versatile shabby chic live–work space.

Cabins don't have to be all wooden logs and rustic styling. Far from it. They also lend themselves to an altogether more romantic and feminine style, as seen on these pages. Take inspiration from this cabin, which belongs to Steph Eley, an antiques dealer based in Oxfordshire, UK specializing in French decorative antiques. It plays multiple roles as an overflow living space, a showroom and somewhere to store her stock.

Steph's interiors style is shabby chic meets French country and the homestead is the perfect example of her look. The planked walls and floors have been painted a soft, chalky white that provides the perfect backdrop for her ever-changing stock of French antiques. Old shutters and doors complete with their original peeling paintwork

are propped up against the walls, while vintage tables, trunks and dressers hold an artful array of enamelware and old galvanized metal buckets and troughs. Carved wooden mirrors and frames add a touch of grandeur to proceedings. It's a treasure trove of vintage delights.

If Steph's country brocante cabin appeals, this look is one that's surprisingly easy to recreate, even in a new-build garden structure. Use a warm white paint for the interior walls, floor and ceiling, then have fun tracking down some vintage French furniture of your own. Prop old doors up against the walls and dress your seating in vintage linen cushions. Having said that, there are plenty of furniture companies out there producing modern items in a shabby chic style and colour palette.

A TREASURE TROVE

Steph Eley's decorative antiques imbue her cabin with a romantic, feminine vibe and bring French style to deepest Oxfordshire (left and opposite). Vintage treasures such as these work well in a rustic-style shed, but will also bring atmosphere and visual interest to the clean white interior of a newly built and painted cabin. The natural weathered wood of the exterior brings to mind the classic settler cabins of New England (below).

A FRENCH-INSPIRED
SUMMER HOUSE

Vintage finds have been used to style this pretty cabin inside and out.

Julie Langley, the owner of this lovely summer house in Surrey, UK, runs Home & Vintage Living, which combines her passion for interiors with carefully curated finds. Home to a constantly changing range of vintage items sourced from French flea markets, Julie's summer house (sourced from Dutch company Tuin) has an elegant, French-inspired theme and, despite its name, is actually used year-round as a spot for entertaining and relaxing.

The cabin has a generous floor plan and contains a deep corner sofa tucked to one side. A white-painted antique dresser/hutch occupies the back wall while a large pedestal table takes centre stage. On the other side, a vintage desk with many drawers for storing all sorts of bits and pieces has been angled under another set of windows with views over the garden, and alongside is a French armoire used to hold vintage trinkets.

The space has a tranquil, calming feel thanks to its muted palette. The walls are whitewashed and the furniture painted in shades of off-white and delicate soft grey.

A double layer of plump cushions made mainly from vintage French linen covers the deep sofa. Fitted seagrass flooring makes the space feel warm and homely, while little nooks house smaller pieces of furniture as well as rustic stools and plenty of freshly picked flowers that add scent as well as a romantic feel. Outside, a classic wooden bistro set painted in a faded pale blue takes pride of place.

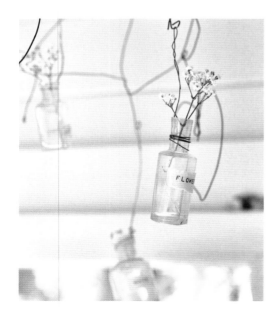

DIY DETAILS
A long, low vintage metal trough has been used as a planter under the double window at the front of the cabin, planted up with white pelargoniums and foxgloves (above). Julie created the delicate wirework chandelier that hangs over the desk by bending rusted wire into shape. Tiny glass bottles are suspended from it (left), each with a word stuck onto it to spell out the Monet quote, 'I must always have flowers'.

FRENCH FANCY

Vintage French items such as armoires, decorative framed mirrors, bistro sets and enamelware can be sourced from Home & Vintage Living or similar companies. Julie trades at local fairs and flea markets besides running her own events. Heading off to France on holiday? Research the area you're visiting so that you can scout out local brocantes or flea markets while you're there.

A WOOD-CLAD
RUSTIC CABIN

This calming garden sanctuary
is its stylist owner's retreat.

This cabin was designed by stylist Jo Rigg for her London garden. Jo's plan utilized an existing brick garage that she inherited with her property. The structure was no longer safe and had an asbestos roof that required expert removal. During this process, Jo's builders informed her that the back wall of the old garage was structurally sound and she decided to construct a cabin on the same spot as the former garage. A timber frame was erected and covered with timber cladding on the exterior, which Jo has stained inky black. The old brick wall inside has been sealed but not repainted, as its aged patina was too attractive to cover. The other interior walls were fashioned from a mix of reclaimed wood planks and recycled corrugated metal sheeting.

Initially, Jo used the cabin as storage space while her house underwent renovations, but as soon as the work was complete, she began to use the cabin as a garden retreat. Now it's put into service for photoshoots, office work and as a wood store for the wood-burning stove in Jo's kitchen. The cabin has power, so a plug-in radiator heats the space during the colder months. The concrete floor – another remnant from the garage – was given a facelift with chalky white floor paint and softened with a jute rug from IKEA. A vintage table and chair create a cute workspace, while a palm leaf wall hanging from Madam Stoltz introduces a natural living vibe.

OUTSIDE STYLE
Outside the cabin, Jo used her styling skills to create a garden display of vintage and reclaimed items. She painted the garden wall black to match the cabin and constructed a bench from old railway sleepers/railroad ties (above). The bamboo poles and string are somewhere to hang paper lanterns on dry days and celebrations. This stylish display sets the scene for the cabin, mixing vintage enamelware and galvanized metal planters with a giant cactus in a basket planter positioned in the centre – perfectly fitting for the hot summer months (left).

INSIDE STYLE

On the walls, reclaimed timber cladding contrasts with the original brick and exposed structural beams (this page). The Madam Stoltz palm leaf wall hanging adds texture, as does a display of dried grasses (above). The cabin doubles as a log store and Jo has made a decorative feature of the wood pile by stacking the logs in an old fruit crate and up against the corrugated metal wall (opposite).

HUTS & OTHER HIDEAWAYS

ESCAPE TO A MOBILE RETREAT

SUMMER CAMP
Head to your own garden hideaway when you feel in need of a summer break (left and opposite). It can also be a sociable spot to hang out. Use your hut as a backdrop for campfire moments and get creative with a barbecued dinner (above).

TINY RETREATS

Sometimes the smallest spaces make the best garden escapes.

Despite their size, tiny garden buildings have bags of potential. Mobile on-wheels structures, as shown on these pages, instantly evoke the free-wheeling charm of the open road and a sense of escape. Shepherds' huts are particularly popular at present, but other movable hideaways such as caravans and camper vans also make great retreats with a laid-back vibe.

If you have a large garden, a hut tucked away in a hidden corner will have secret appeal. In a small garden, create a similar effect by using planting to screen off a tiny hideaway. It will give you a sense of separation, even if the hut is only steps from your back door.

To solve the problem of limited floor space, think about clever small-space solutions. Drop-down shelves or tables can be folded out of the way when not in use, for example. A daybed is ideal for a quick snooze and also offers additional seating when you are entertaining friends. Steph Eley has cleverly converted an old horsebox to create a cosy nook in her Oxfordshire, UK garden (see opposite). She styled the interior with a rustic wood bistro set and positioned a bench against the back wall, softening it up with a chintzy vintage eiderdown. Vintage metal storm lanterns, a fire bowl and a galvanized planter add texture and contrast.

STYLE TIP

Pick chalky white paint for the interior of your hut to keep the space feeling bright and airy (opposite). Outside, you can be more daring. A cheery primrose yellow shade gives this corrugated metal hut heaps of nostalgic charm. The windows and door have been picked out in a bolder shade of the same colour.

ON THE MOVE

Classic camper vans can be given a new lease of life as quirky garden rooms.

If you have vehicular access to your garden, it may be possible to drive (or push) a vehicle into the perfect spot. Parked-up caravans, campers or even decommissioned minivans or buses can become a home office or even guest accommodation. One huge advantage of a mobile garden room is that you can position it to make the most of natural light and existing views, but it's best not to upset the neighbours by parking it too close to your boundary or in their line of sight. Not sure where to source such a vehicle? Try online auction sites, second-hand car dealers or specialist vintage sellers, and if possible view before purchasing.

The blue retro van shown below is fun and quirky, and suits its eclectic homespun decor, featuring patchwork cushions, mismatched floral patterns and multicoloured walls. It can be tempting to gut a vehicle to make room for new furniture and decor, but there may be some elements worth keeping. In the vintage American bus shown opposite, a built-in table and seating were retained and are used as a dining area by the owners. A more dramatic approach was needed to fit in the double bed – the fixed seating was removed, but the space still maintains its school bus charm thanks to the handrails and safety signs. Add your own style by getting creative with vintage wallpaper and soft furnishings. Some of the windows in this bus were left bare to provide uninterrupted garden views, while others were dressed with blinds made from vintage fabrics for a homely feel.

ROOMS ON WHEELS

Short of space? If your garden is large enough, why not convert an old van or even a minibus into a cosy guest house (this page) with no foundations or building work necessary. Of course, an old vehicle will have to be renovated and refurbished to make it fit for guests. This hippie chic van becomes a home from home at the bottom of a garden, kitted out with a comfy built-in sofa bench and a well-stocked kitchenette – this is where I want to have my tea break (opposite)!

CARAVAN STYLE

This pretty caravan was designed by Atlanta Bartlett and Dave Coote. The interior is decked out with vintage accessories set against a backdrop of sage green and white (this page and opposite). It's a luxurious little crash pad with a drop-down shelf that can be used as a desk or dressing table, a double bed and even a roll-top tub. Weekend bags can be stored under the bed and there's lots of handy shelving. It's a lovely place for guests to stay or to escape to for a few hours.

A 1950S
SHOWMAN'S VAN

This vintage van makes me want to run away and join the circus.

Baileys Home is a rustic home and garden emporium housed in a series of old barns and situated on a farm in Ross-on-Wye, UK. It's run by a dynamic designer/maker husband and wife team, Sally and Mark Bailey. You may recognize their names, as this creative couple have authored lots of lovely interiors books – take a look at their Instagram @baileyshome to find out more. I'm a big fan of Mark and Sally's work, and although the store is a six-hour round trip from my home in Surrey, it's always a treat to visit – their recycled homewares, eco ranges and gorgeous collection of gardenalia are all on my wish list. It's a real delight to include their glorious 1950s showman's van here.

Sally and Mark acquired Molly, as they call their vintage van, in a dilapidated state after spotting an advertisement in the window of a local newsagents. The task of restoring it took not far off three years to complete. Built mainly from wood with an aluminium exterior, the couple's first task was to repair the roof and make the van watertight. They then fabricated tongue-and-grove boarding in

their workshop and completely panelled the interior. Finally, a cast-iron Esse Ironheart wood-burning stove and range cooker was installed to heat the van and cook on.

The van is a real home away from home with interior styling in keeping with the Baileys brand, combining rustic details and recycled materials with beautiful artisan wares.

ROOM MATES

The sleeping area of the van features two single beds positioned under the window (opposite). A vintage tea chest serves as a bedside table/nightstand, home to a fan and cool drink in the summer months. Toes are kept warm by the Esse Ironheart wood-burning stove, which is also used for cooking and making hot drinks. Handy wall hooks forgo the need for a bulky wardrobe (left). The exterior of the van is an appealing shade of olive green (above).

MODERN RUSTIC

Mark and Sally Bailey have used their signature simple and unadorned style to kit out the interior of their showman's van. Natural wood flooring made from old floorboards is combined with crisp white tongue-and-groove walls, simple linen textiles and artisan ceramics (this page and opposite).

A TRADITIONAL
SHEPHERD'S HUT

A perfect shepherd's hut tucked away in the corner of the garden.

No longer reserved only for shepherds, these huts have hit the mainstream, making them a much sought-after garden accessory. Originally used by shepherds who needed to spend night after night in the fields during lambing season, these wagons were built on strong axles with cast-iron wheels so that they could be towed from field to field, and feature small windows to allow the shepherd to keep an eye on his flock. In recent years, vintage shepherds' huts have become increasingly desirable as a garden bolt-hole, so finding the genuine article is rare these days, but there are plenty of artisan makers creating bespoke replicas. Modern huts can be tailored to your requirements and often incorporate recycled materials, which retain their vintage charm.

Shepherds' huts can be used for all manner of activities, from painting studios to guest bedrooms and pretty much anything else.

This traditional-style hut owned by Sophie Bateman was built by Roundhill Shepherd Huts, a family business located in West Sussex, UK. It's positioned next to Sophie's vegetable plot in the corner of her gorgeous English country garden. The exterior is clad with painted corrugated iron and it sits on a wooden base on its signature big cast-iron wheels. Sophie has decorated the interior with vintage flair. Reclaimed wooden flooring has been finished with a light limewash, while the vintage French sofa is dressed with a faded floral eiderdown and cushions in natural linen. It's quite roomy – Sophie has even managed to fit in an upright piano plus a corner stove that heats the space on chilly winter days.

COUNTRY STYLE
Wooden steps painted to match the duck-egg blue exterior lead up to a reclaimed stable door, which has been adapted to include a vintage stained glass window panel (left and opposite). The hut has generous windows to make the most of the glorious views of Sophie's country-style garden (above).

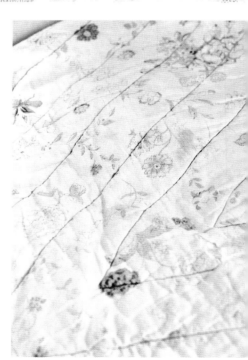

CALM AND COLLECTED

The interior of Sophie's shepherd's hut combines muted tones with vintage finds (this page and opposite). Walls are painted in Great White from Farrow & Ball and offer a simple, elegant backdrop for a glazed cupboard and upright piano. Sophie's desk has a vintage wood tabletop with foldaway legs. The entire design has a restful feel, allowing Sophie to get away from it all just at the end of the garden.

GARDEN STUDIOS & PODS

DESIGN, DECORATION AND STYLING

MODERN PODS

Commission a contemporary structure to give your garden the wow factor.

Modern garden pods have soared in popularity in recent years as homeowners look to their gardens for additional living space. New-build pods often boast architecturally striking designs, like this Escape Pod by Podmakers, a company based in Gloucestershire, UK. Its organic circular form makes me think of an acorn or pine cone. The exterior is clad in cedar shingles and constructed from birch ply and European oak, while the contemporary interior provides a serene spot to work, meditate or socialize. The pod sits on a platform 50cm/1ft 8in above the ground and can rotate to follow the sun (or a chosen view) through its curved windows. It boasts heating, electrics and insulation, making it snug all year round.

It's a good idea to employ a company specializing in contemporary garden rooms and pods to help you design and realize your vision. When it comes to styling the interior, be selective about the furnishings you choose. Quality materials will speak for themselves, while characterful mid-century modern pieces and design classics will fit well. You could even add some tech in the shape of a state-of-the-art wireless music system or the latest coffee machine for a thoroughly modern moment.

CEDAR SHINGLES

Overlapping cedar shingles are an environmentally friendly traditional roofing material and can also be used for wall cladding. Their natural good looks and rich, honeyed hue make them perfect for a garden structure.

MULTIPURPOSE STUDIO

This garden studio by Marc Salamon of London Garden Rooms is a versatile multipurpose space – it's a home office, music studio and hub for laid-back get togethers (this page). Photographer Cathy Pyle sourced a vintage German beer garden folding table and matching benches for her garden room, which she uses as a flexible working space and exhibition venue (opposite above). The surface of the table, once painted yellow, has been worn and weathered by years of use, but the sides still feature the original sunny paint colour.

BACKYARD WORKSPACES

Working from home has never looked so good.

In recent years, there has been a huge trend to utilize space in the garden for a home studio or office. For anyone who currently works perched at the kitchen table or in a spare bedroom, the move to a dedicated workspace outside will physically and mentally separate home and work life. If you already run your own business, work on a freelance basis or want to start up a new enterprise, a garden office can be a game changer – there's no tiring commute to work and you will make savings on renting an office...plus there's the added bonus of working in your own leafy backyard.

   You don't need a huge garden in order to realize this dream, but you will have to tailor the size of your studio or pod to the size of your garden (and to your budget). The office studio shown left has been built at the end of a narrow town garden. The front deck encompasses a raised bed that softens the angles of the structure and offers a pleasant view. To one side, a covered area is home to bikes, garden equipment and the lawn mower.

STYLE TIP

This garden studio has a modern industrial vibe thanks to its recycled corrugated metal exterior and chunky new oak-framed doors and window. It has a sedum-covered green roof, which softens the metal cladding, contributes to the local biodiversity and absorbs rainwater.

PLANTING COMPANIONS

This striking studio, designed by Amos Goldreich Architecture, spans the width of a small city garden (this page and opposite). It's constructed from oak and corrugated metal, which will both weather beautifully over time. The textured cladding was chosen to mirror industrial buildings in the surrounding area. Skylights, a window and glazed door bring ample natural light into the studio. Tailor the planting around a garden studio to suit the environment – in this urban setting, bamboos, cactus and succulents all work perfectly.

HOME FROM HOME

When you need more living space, but don't want to move.

If you feel that you're fast running out of space indoors, a purpose-built garden studio like the one featured on these pages could be the ideal solution. Such a structure provides additional space without the heavy cost of an extension/addition or loft/attic conversion and creates a designated area for whatever you need most in your life – a home office, teen den or yoga studio.

In this London garden, two new buildings have been built opposite each other on a raised area that occupies the bottom of the plot. The large cabin on the right-hand side offers additional living space, while the smaller structure is more akin to a traditional shed and is used for storing garden furniture, equipment and tools. The wide decked space in between acts as an

outdoor dining area during the summer months, with a rustic table in the centre. Clever planting blends the new buildings with their surroundings perfectly. An established climber cloaks the garden wall and draws the eye away from neighbouring buildings, while clusters of vintage galvanized dolly tubs and old buckets soften the new wood of the buildings and hold a mix of fragrant herbs and an olive tree that links the building to the garden.

The interior of the large cabin has been given a cheerfully retro feel, with 1950s-style unfitted cupboards creating a mini kitchenette. The white-painted tongue-and-groove walls and flooring amplify the natural light that floods in through the skylights and keep the interior feeling fresh and modern.

MORE SPACE REQUIRED

A fully functioning kitchen has been installed in this garden studio – somewhere to prepare the meals that are enjoyed under the stars on the adjoining terrace (this page and opposite). All the cabinets are freestanding, which means the space is entirely versatile and can be adapted as and when requirements change. It's sensible to think in a flexible way when constructing a garden building so that it can be used for varying purposes at different life stages.

A CREATIVE GARDEN
RETREAT

Recycled and vintage elements come together to create a garden hideaway.

A brick path leads to a wooden decked area in front of this delightfully rustic garden workspace. It's a creative hub designed and built by the photographic stylist Rose Hammick and her architect husband Andrew. The multipurpose space is larger than it appears from outside and is variously used as a photographic location, a teenage hang-out and a screening room (there's a hidden projector and pull-down screen tucked away in the eaves). There is even enough room for a large desk here – the perfect place to sit and await creative inspiration.

It took the couple more than two years to complete the build. The large reclaimed metal windows and doors originally came from a factory and Rose sourced them via a salvage dealer. The interior of the cabin is clad with reclaimed boards that the couple recycled from more than a hundred pallets – a true labour of love!

Outside, Rose has used a dense array of country garden-style plants to soften the black-stained wooden structure and provide a sense of separation from the house. Not an inch has been

wasted here – on the decking, plant pots vie for space alongside a small decorative tree in a vintage tub. Solar-powered festoon lights and tea lights in metal lanterns illuminate the path and steps that lead up to the cabin. Salvaged materials such as the ones used here lend themselves perfectly to garden structures – not only are they visually attractive, but they are eco-friendly and often cost less too.

CREATIVE STYLE MIX
Old metal-framed windows and doors salvaged from a factory give the building character and work well with the black wood-clad exterior (opposite). The interior has a rustic feel with wall cladding made from recycled wood. There are vintage touches here too, with galvanized metal planters and milk bottle vases. This is a great example of how to mix styles for a unique and stylish design.

HORTICULTURAL HERITAGE

Rose's garden retreat has a recycled vibe, with botanical prints and flower arrangements adding a charming vintage touch (opposite). On her desk, glass bottles hold single stem flowers, and candles in weathered brass lanterns cast a warm glow. Pretty up windowsills in a garden room with a rainbow-hued array of bottles vases filled with garden-grown flowers (above). Love gardening? Create your own horticultural library in your garden room, ready for when you have a moment to yourself (above left). What could be more fitting for the walls of a garden hub than botanical prints, here hung with decorative bulldog clips (left)?

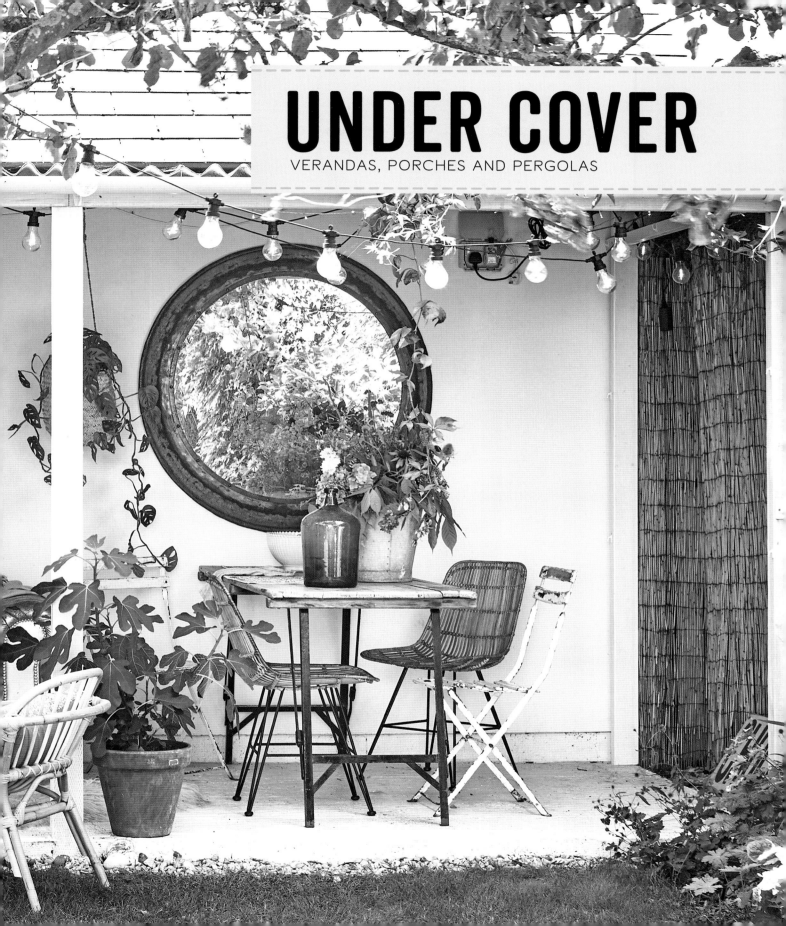

UNDER COVER

VERANDAS, PORCHES AND PERGOLAS

MULTIFUNCTIONAL SPACES

A covered outdoor space will make your garden useful in almost all weathers. At the Worton Organic Garden, a small porch covers the work-cum-prep spot (left). This clapboard house has a veranda with a glazed roof, ideal for soaking up the sun (above). A veranda is a great backdrop for alfresco entertaining (opposite).

VERANDAS & PORCHES

Versatile additions to even the smallest of gardens.

A roofed structure attached to the exterior of a building, such as a veranda or porch, is the ultimate transition between outside and in. It can be partly enclosed or have one or two fixed walls at the ends, leaving just the front open. This type of garden building offers shelter while letting you survey your plot and appreciate all your horticultural endeavours. Anneke and David Blake of Worton Organic Garden in Oxfordshire, UK, built their wooden porch from reclaimed wood, with a sloping roof fashioned from recycled plastic sheeting (see above). The couple use this space for preparing freshly dug organically grown vegetables, and Anneka arranges cut flowers

from the garden here before they are displayed in the shop. Handy hooks have been attached to the wooden structure, allowing the Blakes to store galvanized tubs and watering cans. It's practical and stylish at the same time.

When the weather lends itself to alfresco entertaining, a veranda is the perfect backdrop. When designer and shop owner Catherine Colebrook hosts parties, their mobile pizza oven is dragged out from under the veranda and she sets up a dining table with her assortment of vintage Ercol chairs (see opposite). As the evening draws in, guests like to wend their way back under the veranda to relax in the comfy bamboo chairs.

STYLE TIP

For a chic boho feel, paint the rear wall of your veranda a rich, dark shade. This example belongs to Catherine Colebrook, who chose Railings by Farrow & Ball. It's the perfect backdrop for second-hand rattan and bamboo armchairs, along with accessories by Dassie Artisan from her own store.

NATURALLY NORDIC

At The Norrmans B&B in Denmark, owners Anna and Lars use their open-sided barn for summer parties. With an eye for design, they sourced vintage rattan chairs and have mixed these with simple black metal chairs positioned around a large wooden table (opposite). Inside the barn is a chill-out zone with black-stained wood furniture, a swing seat and oversized paper lanterns that offer a soft ambient light when it gets dark (above). Danish garden designer Dorthe Kvist uses her veranda as somewhere to display her treasured collection of vintage bamboo chairs (left).

PERGOLAS & TERRACES

A versatile addition to any garden, large or small.

A pergola is an open garden structure roofed with slatted beams that support climbing plants and throw dappled shade. Usually attached to the side of a house or garden building, it's the perfect spot for seating or a garden display. Plant something scented to scramble over your pergola, such as a rose, wisteria or honeysuckle, and you will be rewarded with a fragrant, shady spot to hang out in.

I like to use black elements in the garden, as I think the dark background makes greens pop and creates a more contemporary vibe. Staining my shed black was definitely one of my better ideas for our garden. Take inspiration from the Worton Organic Garden, where a vine trails artfully across their black-painted pergola. Underneath stands a French garden table, which when not in use for dining becomes a place for a display – somehow everything looks good against a black backdrop (see opposite). Pergolas can also make interesting walkways linking different buildings – a main house and a garden studio, for example. Again, train a vine or other climbing plant over the framework and hang a mirror on the supporting wall to help bounce the light around.

SHADY SPOTS
Garden rooms don't need to have walls. This wooden arbour at Worton Organic Garden provides a cosy canopy under which to dine (opposite). A pergola built on the side of a building creates a botanical walkway (above left). An outdoor kitchen in Sweden uses a timber pergola for shade (above right).

BOHEMIAN OUTDOOR
LIVING SPACE

Create a relaxing, easy-going space to look out on the garden and lounge in.

It's very handy when you have a relative who's a trained and skilled carpenter, especially when you have visions of creating an outdoor lounge under cover in your back garden. Luckily for interior designer and stylist Dee Campling, her dad is just that. Armed with timber from her local hardware store, Dee sketched a simple veranda design using the wall of her existing garage as a supporting wall, and her lovely dad got straight to work. If you are inspired by Dee's outdoor sitting room and want to build something similar but don't have a handy relative, ask a (recommended) builder or carpenter to give you a quote.

As soon as Dee's new garden hideaway was finished, she decorated the interior by painting the old garage wall white and the new concrete floor of the veranda to match. By keeping the backdrop simple, Dee was free to experiment with furniture and fittings to create different looks. She used two easy fixes to conceal areas that didn't fit with her chosen aesthetic – vintage French doors on a sliding system cover the old door to the garage, while

bamboo-slat screening hides the neighbours' garden and the garage window. The combination of different textures creates plenty of visual interest, and the cosy sofa dressed with cushions and an eiderdown is more than inviting. Dee uses the space as a mini photo studio where she creates images for her clients. When it's not being used for work, it doubles as a place for her three children to hang out, as well as a grown-up retreat for Dee and her husband.

OLD SOFA, NEW LOOK
Before being moved to its new alfresco home, Dee's leather Chesterfield-style sofa was updated with leather spray paint in metallic grey, making it weatherproof (opposite). Twinkling strings of lights illuminate the space after dark, making it usable into the evening (left). I love a mirror in the garden – they double the effect of lush greenery and reflect lots of natural light around the space (above).

ECLECTIC AND BOTANICAL

A vintage railway mirror above this 'fold-away-at-a-moment's-notice' table reflects the garden beyond, while a leafy fig planted in a terracotta pot continues the botanical vibe (opposite). The rattan and the vintage French folding chairs work together to create an eclectic vibe (this page).

SOURCES

BUILDINGS

ALITEX
www.alitex.co.uk
Bespoke Victorian-style greenhouses and conservatories.

DAVE COOTE DESIGN
www.davecoote.com
Bespoke cabins and hideaways made to commission using reclaimed and salvaged materials.

HARTLEY BOTANIC
www.hartley-botanic.co.uk
Traditional greenhouses and glasshouses for growing and preserving plants or simply enjoying as a garden room.

LONDON GARDEN STUDIOS
www.londongardenstudios.co.uk
Modern garden rooms, studios and offices for city gardens.

THE OLD YARD
www.theoldyard.co.uk
Specializing in vintage, industrial and bespoke furniture, lighting and decorative items for your home and garden.

PLANKBRIDGE
www.plankbridge.co.uk
Fine shepherds huts handmade to order in Dorset, UK.

PODMAKERS
www.podmakers.co.uk
Beautiful and unusual outdoor structures.

TUIN
www.tuin.co.uk
Dutch company offering log cabins, gazebos, sheds, fencing, timber, furniture and more.

PAINT

FARROW & BALL
www.farrow-ball.com
British manufacturer of paints and wallpapers; use their Exterior Masonry paints to give outbuildings a new look. My favourite colours are Railings No.31, Great White No.2006 and Calamine No.230.

M&L PAINT
www.mandlpaints.com
M&L (or Marston and Langinger) offer a palette of 130 colours to transform any garden dwelling. My favourites are Graphite Grey, Passiflora and Juniper Green.

PLANTS, SHEDWARE AND GARDEN ACCESSORIES

BURFORD GARDEN COMPANY
www.burford.co.uk
Stylish garden centre with rustic-chic home interiors plus a cafe and art gallery in the heart of the Cotswolds.

DOBBIES GARDEN CENTRES
www.dobbies.com
Look here for seasonal plants, garden accessories and equipment, and on-trend furniture and decorations for the shed and garden.

GARDEN TRADING
www.gardentrading.co.uk
Stylish and elegant garden accessories, garden storage solutions and furniture.

LE PETIT JARDIN
www.le-petit-jardin.com
Gorgeous garden and homeware shop, supplying gardeners and homemakers in and around Tunbridge Wells.

TERRAIN
www.shopterrain.com
Inspiring home and garden decor, furniture, containers and plants. I love following them on Pinterest @terrain

FURNISHINGS

BUNGALOW
www.bungalow.dk
I love their Indian block-printed textiles, linen and velvet cushions, ceramics, baskets, rugs and lanterns.

THE COUNTRY BROCANTE
Griffin House
West Street
Midhurst GU29 9NQ
www.countrybrocante.co.uk
Vintage and antique items for home and garden. They also host fairs and brocantes – a good place for gardenalia.

MADAM STOLTZ
www.madamstoltz.dk
Fantastic textiles, industrial furniture and lamps plus practical and cosy accessories.

TINEKHOME
www.tinekhome.com
Stylish garden furniture and accessories, including lanterns, cushions and bamboo chairs.

PLACES TO VISIT

BAILEYS HOME
Whitecross Farm
Bridstow
Ross-on-Wye
Herefordshire HR9 6JU
+44 (0)1989 561931
www.baileyshome.com
Rustic design store with eco friendly designer household and garden items, furniture, plus an airy tearoom.

LONG BARN
The Old Sheep Fair
Bishops Sutton Road
Alresford SO24 9EJ
+44 (0)1962 738684
www.longbarn.co.uk
Lavender farm with a cafe set within the original vaulted barn. Shop here for fashion as well as home and garden and find unique vintage pieces sourced by @oldabion

PETERSHAM NURSERIES
Church Lane
Off Petersham Road
Richmond
Surrey TW10 7AB
+44 (0)20 8940 5230
petershamnurseries.com
One of my favourite places – an inspiring shop and nursery selling gorgeous gardenalia and plants. Plus there's a tearoom and a restaurant, all set in a magical botanical setting.

ROSENDALS TRÄDGÅRD
Rosendalsvägen 38
115 21 Stockholm
Sweden
+46 8 545 812 70
www.rosendalstradgard.se
Rosendals Garden Foundation is a place for pleasure all year. Their main focus is growing biodynamically but they also have a fabulous shop and cafe situated in large greenhouses.

ROYAL HORTICULTURAL SOCIETY
www.rhs.org.uk
Visit the RHS gardens around the UK for inspiration and their flower shows, which include the prestigious Chelsea Flower Show – the most famous flower show in the UK, held every May since 1912.

BUSINESS CREDITS

SELINA LAKE
Author and stylist
www.selinalake.co.uk
IG and Pinterest: @selinalake
*Pages 12 right, 20 above left,
20 below left, 23 above right,
23 below, 45, 49 right, 60–61,
66–69, 79, 80–81, 159.*

**ALITEX GREENHOUSES
AND CONSERVATORIES**
Torberry Farm
South Harting
Petersfield
Hampshire GU31 5RG
T: +44 (0)1730 826900
E: enquiries@alitex.co.uk
www.alitex.co.uk
*Pages 10 below, 18–19, 40, 47
above right, 72 left, 86–89.*

MARK AND SALLY BAILEY
www.baileyshome.com
*Pages 118 above, 118 below,
119–121.*

SOPHIE BATEMAN
IG: @sophie_b_in_sussex
Pages 122–125.

BEACH STUDIOS
Foster House and Cabins
Designed, built and styled
by Atlanta Bartlett and Dave
Coote
Available to hire for
photography
www.beachstudios.co.uk
*Pages 17 above right, 25 above
right, 33, 116 above, 116 below,
117.*

DAVID AND ANNEKE BLAKE
Worton Organic Garden
Oxfordshire OX29 4SU
www.wortonorganicgarden.com
*Pages 56 centre, 58 above,
142 left, 148.*

DEE CAMPLING
Interior and Event Styling
www.dee-campling.com
*Pages 37 below, 44 above,
140–141, 150–153.*

CATHERINE COLEBROOK
Gifts and homeware shop
Cheltenham
www.catherinecolebrook.com
*Pages 2, 14, 28–29, 50–51, 143,
144–145, 157.*

DOBBIES GARDEN CENTRE
www.dobbies.com
*Pages 6, 20 above right,
22 centre, 52 right, 54.*

STEPHANIE ELEY
IG: @Pearlyhill_
Pages 98–99, 111.

RUSS AND LOUISE GRACE
The Little Red Robin
Artisan garden frames,
plant supports and flowers
www.thelittleredrobin.com
E: info@thelittleredrobin.com
*Pages 39, 56 left, 56 right,
57, 59.*

DORTHE KVIST
Garden designer, author
and blogger
Designer/founder
MELTdesignstudio
T: +45 2615 2906
E: dk@meltdesignstudio.com
www.meltdesignstudio.com
IG: @meltdesignstudio
*Pages 10 above right, 12 left,
13 left, 53, 146 below.*

JULIE LANGLEY
www.homeandvintageliving.
co.uk
Pages 4 left, 90–91, 100–103.

LIGHT LOCATIONS
Location Agency
www.lightlocations.com
*Pages 10 above left, 62–65,
134–135.*

M&L PAINTS
Torberry Farm
South Harting
Petersfield
Hampshire GU31 5RG
T: +44 (0)1730 779911
E: enquiries@mandlpaints.com
www.mandlpaints.com
*Pages 34 above left, 40,
41 right.*

MAMORA ROAD
Available to hire
www.mamoraroad.co.uk
*Pages 5 right, 46 left, 47 above
left, 136–139.*

ANNA AND LARS NORRMAN
The Norrmans Boutique B&B
IG: @thenorrmans
thenorrmans.com
*Pages 28 left, 72 right, 73,
146 above, 147.*

PODMAKERS
Unit 1, The Saw Yard
Yanworth
Gloucestershire GL54 3LJ
T: +44 (0)1285 343016
E: info@podmakers.co.uk
www.podmakers.co.uk
Pages 128–129.

CATHY PYLE PHOTOGRAPHER
www.cathypyle.com
Pages 29, 131 right.

JO RIGG
Home and garden available
to hire.
www.jorigg.co.uk
*Pages 15 left, 20 below right,
22 right, 24 above, 36 right,
37 above, 55, 104–107.*

CLARA SEWELL-KNIGHT
IG: @foundandfavour
*Pages 13 right, 24 below right,
31 below, 34 above right,
52 left.*

DEBBIE SMAIL
IG: @the_bowerbird
*Pages 23 above left, 30 below
left, 31 above, 48 above left,
49 left, 58 below, 108–109, 160.*

**STUDIO GIDEON RUBIN
AND SILIA KA TUNG**
Designer:
Marc Salomon
London Garden Studios
Architect:
Amos Goldreich Architecture
Studio 32, Bickerton House
25 Bickerton Road
London N19 5JT
T: +44 (0)20 7272 6592
E: amos@agarchitecture.net
www.agarchitecture.net
Pages 27, 132–133.

LONDON GARDEN STUDIOS
Marc Salomon
77 Kempe Road
London NW6 6SN
T: +44 (0)7958 511195
E: mail@londongardenstudios.
co.uk
www.londongardenstudios.co.uk
Pages 27, 130–131,132–133.

UNIQUE HOME STAYS
uniquehomestays.com
Page 38.

LENA WALLIN
IG: @lenasskoghem
*Pages 25 left, 30 below right,
82–85.*

PICTURE CREDITS

All photography by Rachel Whiting except where stated.
1 Love Lane Caravans, Cornwall, designed by Anna Bingham and Dan Mullaly/Ph. Debi Treloar; 2 The garden room and shed of Cath Colebrook in Cheltenham, catherinecolebrook.com; 3 The garden of Anna Malm in Sweden; 4 left The home and studio of Julie Langley, homeandvintageliving.co.uk; 4 right Eriksdal Lunden Allotment Gardens, eriksdalslunden.se; 5 left Susannah and David le Mesurier's home in Wales; 5 right location to hire mamoraroad.co.uk; 6 Dobbies Garden Centres, dobbies.com/Ph. Julia Currie; 7 The studio of designer Erika Harberts of mikodesign.nl/Ph. Helen Cathcart; 8–9/Ph. Nicolette Hallett; 10 above left Forest House in Sussex (available for hire through lightlocations.com); 10 above right The home of garden designer and author Dorthe Kvist, meltdesignstudio.com; 10 below left Alitex Greenhouses and Conservatories, alitex.co.uk, styled and photographed by Selina Lake; 10 below right Alitex Greenhouses and Conservatories, alitex.co.uk, styled by Selina Lake/Ph. Julia Currie; 11 An artist's house in the Netherlands; 12 left The home of garden designer and author Dorthe Kvist, meltdesignstudio.com; 12 right styled by Selina Lake at her home; 13 left The home of garden designer and author Dorthe Kvist, meltdesignstudio.com; 13 right The family home and garden of Clara Sewell-Knight; 14 The garden room and shed of Cath Colebrook in Cheltenham, catherinecolebrook.com; 15 left The garden of Jo Rigg, photographic stylist, jorigg.co.uk; 15 right The Suffolk studio of Belle Daughtry, @just_belle/Ph. Ben Edwards; 16 Stiftelsen Rosendals Trädgård rosendalstradgard.se; 17 above left Arendal Creamics, arendal-creamics.com/Ph. Debi Treloar; 17 above right Foster House, the family home of Atlanta Bartlett and Dave Coote, available to hire for photography through beachstudios.co.uk/Ph. Polly Wreford; 17 below The garden of Viktoria Johansson of lillagrona.se; 18–19 Alitex Greenhouses and Conservatories, alitex.co.uk, styled by Selina Lake/Ph. Julia Currie; 20 above left and below left Styled by Selina Lake at her home; 20 above right Dobbies Garden Centre, dobbies.com, styled by Selina Lake/Ph. Julia Currie; 20 below right The garden of Jo Rigg, photographic stylist, jorigg.co.uk; 21 Susannah and David le Mesurier's home in Wales; 22 left The garden of Anna Malm in Sweden; 22 centre Dobbies Garden Centre, dobbies.com, styled by Selina Lake/Ph. Julia Currie; 22 right The garden of Jo Rigg, photographic stylist, jorigg.co.uk; 23 above left The garden of Debbie Smail, Sussex; 23 above right and below Styled by Selina at her home; 24 above The garden of Jo Rigg, photographic stylist, jorigg.co.uk; 24 below left Stiftelsen Rosendals Trädgård, rosendalstradgard.se; 24 below right The home and garden of Clara Sewell-Knight; 25 left The home and garden of Lena Wallin in Sweden; 25 above right Foster House, designed by Dave Coote and Atlanta Bartlett. Available for hire beachstudios.co.uk/Ph. Polly Wreford; 25 below right Stiftelsen Rosendals Trädgård, rosendalstradgard.se; 26 above Susannah and David le Mesurier's home in Wales;

26 below left Interior design by Beth Dadswell of imperfectinteriors.co.uk; 26 below right Susannah and David le Mesurier's home in Wales; 27 Studio Gideon Rubin and Silia Ka Tung; 28 left The Norrmans Boutique B&B, Denmark; 28 right /Ph.Mark Scott; 28–29 The garden room and shed of Cath Colebrook in Cheltenham catherinecolebrook.com; 29 The summerhouse of photographer Cathy Pyle, cathypyle.com; 30 above Susannah and David le Mesurier's home in Wales; 30 below left The garden of Debbie Smail, Sussex; 30 below right The home and garden of Lena Wallin in Sweden; 31 above The garden of Debbie Smail, Sussex; 31 below The family home and garden of Clara Sewell-Knight; 32 above Barefoot Glamping, barefoot-glamping.co.uk/Ph. Debi Treloar; 32 below left The home and shop of Katarina von Wowern of minaideer.se; 32 below right J.Morgan Puett/Ph. Simon Upton; 33 Foster Cabins, designed by Atlanta Bartlett and Dave Coote and available for hire through beachstudios.co.uk/Ph. Polly Wreford; 34 above left M&L Paints, mandlpaints.com/Ph. Julia Currie; 34 above right The family home and garden of Clara Sewell-Knight; 34 below left Love Lane Caravans, Cornwall, designed by Anna Bingham and Dan Mullaly/Ph. Debi Treloar; 34 below right Bellevue Homestead, The National Trust, Queensland/Ph. James Merrell; 35 The garden of Viktoria Johansson of lillagrona.se; 36 The home of Rick Livingston and Jim Brawders at Quogue, New York on Long Island/Ph. Earl Carter; 36 right The garden of Jo Rigg, photographic stylist, jorigg.co.uk; 37 above The garden of Jo Rigg, photographic stylist, jorigg.co.uk; 37 below The garden room of Dee Campling in Cheltenham, dee-campling.com; 38 Apifera, a stone cottage in Herefordshire available to rent through uniquehomestays.com; 39 The home and garden of Russ and Louise Grace; 40 Alitex Greenhouses and Conservatories, alitex.co.uk and M&L Paints, mandlpaints.com/Ph. Julia Currie; 41 left Love Lane Caravans, Cornwall designed by Anna Bingham and Dan Mullaly/Ph. Debi Treloar; 41 right M&L Paints, mandlpaints.com/Ph.Julia Currie; 42 left Susannah and David le Mesurier's home in Wales; 42 right The home and garden of Catarina Persson in Sweden; 43 The home of Debora Treep and Jan van Pelt in the Netherlands; 44 above The garden room of Dee Campling in Cheltenham, dee-campling.com; 44 below/Ph. Edina van der Wyck; 45 Styled by Selina Lake at her home; 46 left location to hire mamoraroad.co.uk; 46 right The garden of Viktoria Johansson of lillagrona.se; 47 above left location to hire, mamoraroad.co.uk; 47 above right Alitex Greenhouses and Conservatories alitex.co.uk, styled by Selina Lake/Ph. Julia Currie; 47 below left Lindeborgs Eco Retreat, designed and owned by Julia and Carl Lindeborg, lindeborgs.com; 47 below right Available for hire, debitreloar.com/Ph. Debi Treloar; 48 above left The garden of Debbie Smail, Sussex; 48 below left/Ph.Tom Leighton; 48 right The garden of Susann Larsson in Lomma, Sweden; 49 left The garden of Debbie Smail, Sussex; 49 right styled by Selina Lake at her home; 50–51 The garden

room and shed of Cath Colebrook in Cheltenham, catherinecolebrook.com; 52 left The family home and garden of Clara Sewell-Knight; 52 right Dobbies Garden Centres, dobbies. com, styled by Selina Lake/Ph. Julia Currie; 53 The home of garden designer and author Dorthe Kvist, meltdesignstudio. com; 54 Dobbies Garden Centres, dobbies.com, styled by Selina Lake/Ph. Julia Currie; 55 The garden of Jo Rigg, photographic stylist, jorigg.co.uk; 56 left The home and garden of Russ and Louise Grace; 56 centre Worton Organic Garden Oxfordshire, owned by Anneke and David Blake; 56 right The home and garden of Russ and Louise Grace; 57 The home and garden of Russ and Louise Grace; 58 above Worton Organic Garden Oxfordshire, owned by Anneke and David Blake; 58 below The garden of Debbie Smail, Sussex; 59 The home and garden of Russ and Louise Grace; 60–61 styled by Selina Lake/ Ph. Sussie Bell; 62–65 Available to hire lightlocations.com; 66–69 styled by Selina Lake at her home; 70–71 Stiftelsen Rosendals Trädgård, rosendalstradgard.se; 72 left Alitex Greenhouses and Conservatories, alitex.co.uk/Barbara Brooks Garden Design/Ph. Chris Warren; 72 right The Norrmans Boutique B&B, Denmark; 73 The Norrmans Boutique B&B, Denmark; 74 Stiftelsen Rosendals Trädgård, rosendalstradgard.se; 75 The home and shop of Katarina von Wowern of minaideer.se; 76 The home and garden of Wil and Bertus Aldershof-Koch, Smidse Voorstonden Bed and Breakfast; 77 above left and below right The home of Marie Emilsson of trip2garden.se; 77 above right The home and shop of Katarina von Wowern of minaideer. se; 78 Stiftelsen Rosendals Trädgård, rosendalstradgard.se; 79 Styled by Selina Lake at her home; 80–81 Styled by Selina Lake/Ph. Sussie Bell; 82–85 The home and garden of Lena Wallin in Sweden; 86–89 Alitex Greenhouses and Conservatories, alitex. co.uk, styled by Selina Lake/Ph. Julia Currie; 90–91 The home and studio of Julie Langley, homeandvintageliving.co.uk; 92 centre Debi Treloar's home, available to hire at debitreloar.com/ Ph. Debi Treloar; 92 right and 93 The family home of designer and shop owner An-Magritt Moen in Norway/Ph. Debi Treloar; 94–95 The home of the designers Stine and Henrik Busk/ Ph. Debi Treloar; 96 below and right The home of the designers Stine and Henrik Busk/Ph. Debi Treloar; 98–99 The homestead of Stephanie Eley in Oxfordshire @pearlyhill_/ Ph. Ben Edwards; 100–103 The home and studio of Julie Langley, homeandvintageliving.co.uk; 104–107 The garden of Jo Rigg, photographic stylist, jorigg.co.uk; 108–109 The garden of Debbie Smail, Sussex; 110 left The family home of Sarah Mark Benton in Rye/Ph. Polly Wreford; 110 right Love Lane Caravan Park, Cornwall, barefootcornwall.com/Ph. Debi Treloar; 111 The homestead of Stephanie Eley in Oxfordshire @pearlyhill_/Ph. Ben Edwards; 112 /Ph. Simon Brown; 113–115 Love Lane Caravans, Cornwall, designed by Anna Bingham and Dan Mullaly/Ph. Debi Treloar; 116 above and 117 The White House, owned by Paul Burgess, designed by Dave Coote and Atlanta Bartlett and available for lets and photography at beachstudios. co.uk/Ph. Polly Wreford; 116 below Forest House, the family home of Atlanta Bartlett and Dave Coote, available for hire for photography at beachstudios.co.uk/Ph. Polly Wreford; 118 above The home of Mark and Sally Bailey/Ph. Mark Bailey; 118 below–121 The home of Mark and Sally Bailey/Ph. Debi Treloar; 122–125 The home of Sophie Bateman and family in Sussex @sophie_b_in _ sussex/Ph. Ben Edwards; 126–127 The home of George Lamb in London, designed by Maria Speake of Retrouvius/Ph. Debi Treloar; 128–129 podmaker.co.uk/Ph. Tim Brotherton; 130–131 Designed by Marc Salomon of London Garden londongardenstudios.co.uk/Ph. Mark Tamer; 131 right The studio of photographer Cathy Pyle/Ph. Cathy Pyle; 132–133 Studio Gideon Rubin and Silia Ka Tung; 134–135 lightlocations. com; 136–139 location to hire at mamoraroad.co.uk; 140–141 The garden room of Dee Campling in Cheltenham, dee-campling. com; 142 left Worton Organic Garden Oxfordshire, owned by Anneke and David Blake; 142 right The Linen Shed, boutique B&B near Whitstable, Kent www.linenshed.com/Ph. Catherine Gratwicke; 143 The garden room and shed of Cath Colebrook in Cheltenham, catherinecolebrook.com; 144–145 The garden room and shed of Cath Colebrook in Cheltenham, catherinecolebrook.com; 146 above The Norrmans Boutique B&B, Denmark; 146 below The home of garden designer and author Dorthe Kvist, meltdesignstudio.com; 147 The Norrmans Boutique B&B, Denmark; 148 Worton Organic Garden Oxfordshire, owned by Anneke and David Blake; 149 The garden of Anna Malm in Sweden; 150–153 The garden room of Dee Campling in Cheltenham, dee-campling.com; 157 The garden room and shed of Cath Colebrook in Cheltenham, catherinecolebrook. com; 159 Styled by Selina Lake at her home; 160 The garden of Debbie Smail, Sussex.

INDEX

Page numbers in italic refer to the illustrations

ACKNOWLEDGMENTS

Shed Style has been such a great project to work on. I've loved styling and shooting new creative spaces, revisiting sheds, cabins and greenhouses from previous books, and including commissions undertaken for commercial clients such as M&L Paints, Alitex Greenhouses and Dobbies Garden Centres.

Thank you to my publishers for commissioning my tenth book, and for the team effort to get the book finished. Huge thanks go to all the shed owners who welcomed me into their lovely gardens and to the talented photographers I have the pleasure of working with and calling friends: Rachel Whiting, Debi Treloar, Sussie Bell and Julia Currie. Also, thanks to the photographers I'm yet to have the pleasure of working with who supplied lovely images for the book.

Big thanks to my styling buddy Sarah Prall @sarahjanelane, who is always smiling on our photoshoots and providing the perfect props at exactly the right moment. Thanks especially for all your hard work and dedication to our Alitex project at the RHS Chelsea Flower Show 2019.

I'd also like to say a massive thank you to everyone who supports my work via social media – I always appreciate your lovely comments, likes and follows. I would love to see your garden buildings if you have been inspired by *Shed Style*. Please tag me @selinalake and use the hashtags #shedstyle and #shedware

Finally, thanks to my husband Dave and my family for always supporting me. X